Suzy has been a mentor and friend to me since I was twelve years old. She is a teacher by nature, and her credibility is rooted in authenticity and wisdom. Suzy offers hope as her deepest, most genuine thoughts from childhood collaborate with her life experience, knowledge, wisdom, and humor.

—Stephanie Smith, Gotee recording artist

Most of my career for the last eight years has been working with teenage girls, and the saddest reality about the teen years is that we all struggle with insecurities, for different reasons and in different ways (even those girls we thought were beautiful and always put together perfectly). I'm so glad that books like Secret Diary Unlocked: My Struggle to Like Me are being written. Being willing to be honest about our fears and mistakes and insecurities helps the process seem less foreign and scary to the girls going through it now. Secret Diary is written in an honest and fun way that I think any female will enjoy . . . so if you're a girl shopping for a new read, pick this one!!

—Tricia Brock, SuperChick

# SECRET DIARY UNLOCKED

## MY STRUGGLE TO LIKE ME

### Suzy Weibel

**Moody Publishers**

CHICAGO

© 2007 by
SUZY WEIBEL

All Scripture quotations, unless otherwise indicated, are taken from the *Holy Bible, New International Version®*. NIV®. Copyright © 1973, 1978, 1984 by International Bible Society. Used by permission of Zondervan. All rights reserved.
Scripture quotations marked TNIV are taken from the *Holy Bible, Today's New International Version* TNIV®. Copyright© 2001, 2005 by International Bible Society. Used by permission of Zondervan. All rights reserved.

Editor: Pam Pugh
Book cover/interior design: Julia Ryan / www.DesignByJulia.com
Original cover image: JupiterImages, www.comstock.com
Feathery doodle: Dara Lowry

Library of Congress Cataloging-in-Publication Data

Weibel, Suzy.
    Secret diary unlocked : my struggle to like me / by Suzy Weibel.
    p. cm.
    Includes bibliographical references.
    ISBN 978-0-8024-8079-8
    1. Teenage girls--Religious life. 2. Self-acceptance in adolescence. 3. Self-acceptance--Religious aspects--Christianity.
I. Title.
BV4551.3.W45 2007
248.8'33--dc22

2007008721

ISBN: 0-8024-8079-9
ISBN-13: 978-0-8024-8079-8

We hope you enjoy this book from Moody Publishers. Our goal is to provide high-quality, thought-provoking books and products that connect truth to your real needs and challenges. For more information on other books and products written and produced from a biblical perspective, go to www.moodypublishers.com or write to:

Moody Publishers
820 N. LaSalle Boulevard
Chicago, IL 60610

5 7 9 10 8 6 4

*Printed in the United States of America*

# CONTENTS

Foreword by Dannah Gresh

## Foreword By Dannah Gresh

I couldn't believe it.
Another e-mail.
They'd been coming all week long.

"That red-headed drummer in the band was really cool. She ministered to me a lot."

She hadn't spoken one word from stage all weekend long.
They didn't even know her name.
But God had done something through her.
Something powerful.
Just by her presence at one of our Pure Freedom events back in 2002, Suzy Weibel had been a conduit of God's power to a large handful of girls. I wondered what would happen if they actually knew her name . . . could hear her heart. I decided to dive right in. I called "that red-headed drummer" the next day.
"Suzy, would you mind doing a little teaching at the next event?"
"I wouldn't mind at all," she answered.
I gave her an open slate to speak on whatever was on her heart.
She showed up at the next event armed with her drumsticks, a new hair color, and her 7th grade diary. When it came time for her to share, the audience was quickly brought into a place of hilarious laughter as Suzy just let her junior high school heart hang out for everyone to see. Her diary wasn't funny because she's a comedian, though she can certainly deliver a laugh line. Her diary was funny to every girl in the room

because every girl's teenaged diary sounded something like Suzy's.

Guys.

Fights with girlfriends.

Guys.

Depression over looks.

Guys.

A day when you wanted to "just die."

Guys.

The latest fashion or music crazes.

Did I mention guys?

After the laughter, Suzy quickly brought us all to tears we she journeyed with us to our deepest places of vulnerability and need. And as quickly as she took us there, she took us to the throne of God for truth and healing. Girls knelt before God. Tears flowed. Hearts were healed.

Suzy has since become my main partnering teacher as we travel around the country doing Pure Freedom events. I continue to see that she's a uniquely powerful teacher. If I didn't love her so much and believe in her so much, I might be jealous at the wild applause and cheering that occurs nearly every single time our team says good-bye on Saturday night.

All of our names are spoken.

They clap for all of us.

They scream with love and adoration for Suzy.

She's reached a place in today's teen girls that deeply needs healing.

Come see for yourself!

CHAPTER 1

## IT WAS A GOOD YEAR

**THE YEAR WAS 1979.** As far as 13-year-old girls go, this really should have been what they call a "banner year"—one of the best. I had been at this same school for six years now. I knew the ins and outs, I was fairly popular, I earned good grades, I was always one of the first chosen for teams at recess. My family vacations in 1979 included trips to Israel and Egypt as well as the Caribbean island of Grand Cayman. What was not to love?

Me. I was not to love.

My hair was curly and never cut right. I couldn't wear it long like all of my friends because it would frizz out and I'd end up looking like Bozo the Clown. I wore it in pigtails in second and third grade, but a mature fourth grader can't really do that. Besides, Maureen Butler had thought for two full years that I was an Indian princess. I didn't want to be an Indian princess. So by middle school, my hair was really "out there" —like Lisa Simpson, but not so neatly drawn.

One of my nicknames was "Piranha," given to me by a guy whose nickname was "Carrot Top." His nickname came, of course, from the fact that he had a shock of red hair. Mine was due to the fact that the only thing more noticeable than the huge space between my two front teeth was the fact that I was missing the next two required teeth in a full set (called the incisors—I know this because my dad was a dentist), but I *had* been blessed with two very pronounced canine teeth, razor sharp, one on each side of my mouth. Perhaps I exaggerate that a bit, but when a 13-year-old girl is dying to make an impression on the guys, this is *not* what she wants to see when she smiles at herself in the mirror.

"YOU KNOW, DEARIE, VERTICAL STRIPES ARE MUCH MORE FLATTERING. EVER TRY BLACK? IT'S A VERY SLIMMING COLOR."

Shopping for clothes was a nightmare. I hated it. I was constantly between sizes and had the kind of figure that wasn't really even a shape at all. I was the kind of girl that sales ladies would smile at kindly and say, "You know, Dearie, vertical stripes are much more flattering. Ever try black? It's a very slimming color." Even when I was a junior in college and making, I thought, a nice impression on a very cute scuba diving instructor, he brought home the truth I had lived with for so many years when he said (to my *mother* of all people), "She'll be a very pretty woman when she loses some of that baby fat." I think that was supposed to be a compliment.

The reason I was one of the first chosen for teams at recess is because I was fairly athletic, but not much of a threat to the guys in the girlfriend department. I was like a sister, they told me. I was also picked first for square dancing. See, if they picked the cute girls, those girls might get the wrong idea . . . or the right idea. Either one was embarrassing for the boys. And they couldn't pick the "outcasts" for obvious reasons. So I was the best choice. Somehow this didn't make me feel any better.

I was forever doing stupid things. On the infamous Israel/Egypt trip my tour group was dining at a restaurant in Old Jerusalem when I decided I needed to visit the little girls' room. My memory of this event may be a bit muddled by time, but this is the chain of events as I recall them: There were no other 13-year-old girls (or even 11-year-olds or a 15-year-old) to accompany me to the bathroom, leaving me to attempt this adventure all alone. This was uncomfortable territory to begin with—having to go it alone—but to make matters worse, the signs on the bathroom doors were not accompanied by any "courtesy English." I don't know about you, but my Hebrew is a little shaky. In America this would not pose too great a problem—we'd simply look at the picture on the bathroom door. I think you could do this in most European countries as well. However, in Jerusalem they must have really wished to preserve the Old World feel, because I insist to this day that both doors had pictures of people with robes on . . . dresses as far as I could tell. I went in one and began to do my business, wondering as I entered if *all* ladies' rooms in Israel had such funny-looking toilets. Before long I was not the only one in the bathroom. Someone in the stall next to me was—now this was odd—pointing his feet in the wrong direction, and they were *big* feet, too. In a blind rush I grabbed my purse and flew out of that bathroom so fast . . . So fast that I did not realize until returning to the table that I had grabbed, in fact, an extra roll of toilet paper and not my purse. The story does have a happy ending, however. I convinced a 16-year-old guy (who later held my hand, but that's for another chapter) to return to the men's room and retrieve my purse. The entire tour group greeted him with cameras, like Hollywood paparazzi, as he exited the men's room carrying my purse!

It was the year that all of my classmates started "going together." I don't know what happened. One year earlier, boys weren't very interesting to any of us. We played together when we had to—I loved sports, so boys were always good for that—but we were more than content to go our separate ways most of the time. Take square dancing for example—back in the "olden days," schools would frequently have the older grades participate in square dancing once a week or so. I think it was to foster listening skills and cooperation, as well as to teach manners, because square dance partners must bow and curtsy to each another. It was pretty gross to have to "swing your partner" in sixth grade, and I think the boys felt the same way. But in seventh grade, selecting someone as a square dance partner was as good as giving one of those notes that say, "I like you. Do you like me? Check yes or no," to someone.

As I've already mentioned, being the "safe" square dance choice was not my preference. I wanted to be noticed. I wanted someone to like me, to ask my friends if they thought I'd "go" with him. I wanted to fit in and be like my friends. But I didn't. I couldn't. Not in this area. They were light-years ahead of me in looks, in fashion, in cuteness. I wasn't sure what I'd have to do or how I'd have to change to become one of the girls all the guys liked, but I was willing to do whatever it took—even if it meant rejecting the way God had created me. I'd do anything. Anything . . .

February 26: My one and only hope is now gone. I was just beginning to like Dan B., but he likes Steph. If she starts going with him I'll croak. I know I'll never have a boyfriend. I feel like crying. MAYBE I WILL.

March 13: It should have been good (today) because we went roller skating. But I had a rotten time. You'd think that with three single, good looking guys there, one would ask me to skate. Oh, but no, Sue's too ugly to even be seen with. And I don't usually fall.

Well I went on my can three times. I was trying to show off. And school was even worse. What a drag.

*May 14: Dan was going to ask me again, but Tanyer and all those creeps got their big noses into it and embarrassed him out of it. I'm tired of being a big fat ▓▓▓▓ :: and I want someone, anyone to ask me! I'm desperate!!!*

**GOD'S DIARY**

I don't think I'm alone. I don't think I'm the only girl who has looked day after day at her reflection in the mirror, hating what she sees, unsure that she will ever be loved. In fact, I've never met a woman or girl who has said, "Really? You didn't like yourself? Hmmmm, I've always been quite pleased with myself." It just doesn't happen. There are a lot of theories on why this is so—we'll take a look at several of them together in this book—but the primary reason is Satan:

"Be alert and of sober mind. Your enemy the devil prowls around like a roaring lion looking for someone to devour. Resist him, standing firm in the faith, because you know that your fellow believers throughout the world are undergoing the same kind of sufferings." (1 Peter 5:8-9 TNIV)

There are a couple of important things I want you to see here. First, the Devil is your enemy, and he wants you destroyed. Another word for "enemy" is "adversary." In the Greek, this meant "one that speaks against another."[1] He speaks against you. What does he say? In my case he said things like:

You're fat. You're ugly. No one will ever love you. You are a freak. It's no wonder they don't want to hang around with you. You aren't worth it.

And how interesting that he speaks those lies right into our own ears! He didn't turn my friends against me, he didn't make me unappealing to the boys, he didn't alter my appearance in any way . . . but he did much worse. He whispered lies to me that I believed, that I embraced, and that I used as a basis for making decisions for many years to come. So why does this destroy us?

A theologian by the name of Matthew Henry said this about Satan: Satan's goal with Christians is to get them thinking so much about their suffering and their bad fortune that they will use whatever is bad in their life as an excuse to refuse or deny God.[2] So if Satan can get us believing all of the negative things we say and think about ourselves—sometimes even the mean things that others say about us—then he's on his way to victory.

The second thing I want you to see in 1 Peter 5:8-9 is this: Girls throughout the world are undergoing the same kind of sufferings. You are not alone! This is the first time I have written down most of these thoughts. But I have spoken them dozens of times to thousands of girls. I always see heads bobbing up and down in complete understanding; sometimes girls are so eager to show their agreement that they are in danger of crossing the fine line between head nodding and head banging. Yeah—I feel really crummy about myself, too! Yeah—I wish I was anyone but me! Some are astounded to see other girls—girls they consider to be beautiful and popular—weeping as they encounter God's unconditional love and acceptance for the first time. You are not the only one who has been lied to, and you are not the only one who hates what she sees in that mirror.

December 22: Beth got me a really flip-out mirror with "You're Gorgeous" on it (since I'm always putting myself down.)

January 14, '80: I don't think Beth's (You're Gorgeous) mirror is helping my complex any. It keeps getting shattered when I go to the Roller Dome. I know I'm not UGLY, but there's something about me that guys don't like...

# MY STRUGGLE

Write an honest evaluation of your
feelings about YOU. While you're at
it . . . how do you think your friends
feel about themselves?

CHAPTER 2

## MY WORLD:

I don't want to sound like those grand-parents who are always saying, "When I was your age I had to walk three miles to school, barefoot, all uphill . . ." but I can understand why grandparents make those kinds of statements. When I begin a serious recall of my child-hood, there are huge differences between then and now!

For instance, let's consider television, of which I was a major connoisseur in seventh grade. I had three net-works to view, plus PBS, but PBS was always fuzzy and it was boring, so I didn't even consider it to be an option. Cable television didn't become available in my neighbor-hood until later in my high school years, but I sure was jealous of the (very few) people I knew who had it. The Fox network simply didn't exist yet.

I remember having black-and-white televisions in the kitchen and den. Our color television was in the basement, and it had a pretty sweet, bubble-like 20-inch screen. Although remote controls were invented during World War II, until the 1980s you had to buy a certain kind of television if you wanted a remote control, and my parents weren't that interested in being on the cutting edge of technology. So (here's my grandma impersonation) *I had to walk all the way across the room* if I wanted to change the television station to one of the two other available stations. Occasionally the main knob of the TV would snap off, and we'd have to keep needle-nosed pliers on the top of the television set so that we could change channels. I guess one good thing I can say about 1979 television is that *TV Guide* sure was an uncomplicated read!

My family did have one piece of cutting-edge technology that a lot of my friends didn't have. In 1972 a really cool arcade game called Pong had been introduced, and as soon as a home system was available (it was called Odyssey) my family purchased one. We had three or four games that had to be loaded via huge cartridges, and that would only provide a black-and-white version of the game on the screen. To add color, we'd have to put something like cellophane on the outside of the television screen where it would stay attached due to static cling. My brothers and I spent countless hours playing this fascinating game . . . Pong was our entire arcade world.

There were no personal computers. In fact, my *typewriter* went through several stages of improvement before I got my first PC . . . which was *long* after I was out of college. I made it through the entirety of college, as a matter of fact, without using a single computer.

So what in the world did we do for entertainment? Roller-skating was probably the biggest attraction for my friends and me in 1979. We had a big rink in town cleverly called The Roller Dome, and I think I was there every weekend throughout middle school. There were no roller blades yet, just the old-fashioned four-wheel kind of

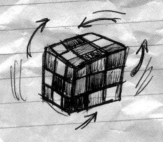

PRESIDENT: Jimmy Carter

GOOGLE THIS HISTORIC EVENT: Iranian hostage crisis

Nobel Peace Prize: Mother Teresa of Calcutta

SPORTS: Pittsburgh won both the World Series and the Super Bowl

MUSIC: First mainstream rap album . . . Sugar Hill Gang's "Rapper's Delight," album of the year . . . "Saturday Night Fever" by the Bee Gees

BIG MOVIES: Apocalypse Now, Kramer vs. Kramer, Breaking Away

JOHN WAYNE, once the most recognizable movie star in America, died in 1979.

BIG TV SHOWS:
Three's Company
Laverne and Shirley
Mork & Mindy
Happy Days
Angie
60 Minutes
M*A*S*H
The Ropers
Charlie's Angels
All in the Family

## Did you know?

At around midnight each night, the networks would each telecast a picture of a waving American flag and play the national anthem, and then the television would simply go to fuzz until sometime the next morning.

skates. It didn't get any better on a Friday night than skating around in a big circle, doing the hand motions to "YMCA" and hoping that foxy guy would ask you to skate. (Guys weren't "hot" back then, by the way. They were "foxes." Some of the biggest foxes of my day were Scott Baio, Erik Estrada, David and Sean Cassidy, Leif Garrett, and Richard Thomas. Go ahead. Look them up online and have a good laugh at my expense.)

The neighborhood park was a big deal—maybe it still is today. We played a lot of politically incorrect games like "Smear the Queer" and "Suicide," but nobody thought those were bad names. We rode our bikes, played tackle football, went sledding and ice-skating in the winter, climbed trees and jumped out of them, and my house happened to have a swimming pool that was a big draw as well. There was a big hill in my neighborhood that every kid had fallen down at least once while trying to ride their bike with no hands.

I read a lot as a kid, and that continued all through . . . well, I still read a lot. I remember my tenth grade geometry teacher getting very frustrated with me because I'd hide a novel under my desk during her class. She had the cutest southern accent. "Miss Dunton, if you don't put that book away in my class I'll skin your hide, put you ten feet under, and make you wish you had!" I loved reading novels, historical fiction, biographies, memoirs . . . but my favorite thing to do was curl up with a bag of Pixie Sticks in my mom's good chair with a pile of *Richie Rich* or *Archie* comic books. This would account for my serious nature and impressive vocabulary today.

Maybe the thing you can identify with the most is "hanging out." We called it that even in 1979, and it was a huge part of my junior high and high school years. If I was awake, I wanted to be with my friends. Parties were always something to get excited about, and every weekend I either had a friend sleep over or I went to someone else's house. If I could get my mom to let me have two or three friends spend the night, it was even better. And boys—well, they were probably my number one source of entertainment in

1979. My husband says I was shallow. I say to him, "Hey, I'd love to read *your* seventh grade diary, if it isn't too smeared from all the drool." And then he chases me around the kitchen.

## YOUR WORLD

Perhaps the greatest difference between my world and yours is in the arena of safety. We played outside until well after dark—in the summer we didn't have to be in until 9 or 10, and my parents never worried about where I was or what I was doing. I guess that has changed a lot over the years.

In your world there is more than just a general need to be careful. There is a need to be careful with who you know, where you hang out, and who you date. You are faced with a lot of scary statistics such as:

Around 2 of every 1000 children in the United States were said to have experienced sexual assault in 2003 according to child protective service agencies.[1]

Between 20% and 25% of college women in the U.S. reported being the victim of completed or attempted rape in 2000.[2] One in six women (17%) and one in thirty-three men (3%) reported experiencing an attempted or completed rape at some time in their lives.[3]

Investigators of two murder cases, those of 14-year-old Judy Cajuste in New Jersey and 15-year-old Kayla Reed in California, are considering the probability that MySpace.com was the primary connection between the girls and their murderers.[4]

Entertainment content is unbelievably different, too. Was I exposed to suggestive images and sexual innuendo when I was thirteen? Yes. But not in the measure you are exposed today. Look at these numbers:

The average American adolescent will view nearly 14,000 sexual references per year.[5]

"The Center for Media and Public Affairs' new study found that sexual content is featured once every four minutes on network TV, with 98% of all sexual content having no subsequent physical consequences, 85% of sexual behavior having no lasting emotional impact, and that nearly 75% of the participants in sexual activity were unmarried."[6]

Or how about this groundbreaking news from USA Today: "The more sex-oriented scenes (teens see), the more likely they (are) to become sexually active."[7]

There were no parental advisory stickers on albums . . .
We didn't have CDs or iPods, you know! My teen magazines
contained articles telling me what my crushes liked to eat
and what they thought a perfect date would be. It was worth-
less fluff, but I never could have imagined then what the
content of teen magazines would be like today! I guess that's
why we love time-travel movies and things like *Freaky Friday*.
It's such fun to look at different worlds.

The greatest difference in our worlds has to be the
technology, though. What would someone from the past
think if they visited us today? Is it possible they could keel
over from shock? You have become accustomed to the world
at your fingertips. You have grown up on the Internet where
for just a few dollars a month you can have access to more
information than a library could ever hold. You can shop
from home and have deliveries brought to your door. You
can watch pandas at the National Zoo via a live camera,
download movies from your phone line into your TV or
computer, and observe the funeral of Pope John Paul II
live from Italy. You can put thousands of songs on your
iPod, call everyone on your phone plan for free, and instant
message dozens of friends simultaneously. You create and
exchange information with people from all over the
world . . . all without the U.S. Postal Service.

I'd be willing to bet, however, that despite the differences
in styles, fads, safety, entertainment, and technology, my
childhood was still similar to yours. My mom and I sometimes
got along and sometimes we didn't. I was asked to do chores
around the house, I tried to get out of them, and sometimes
I was grounded as a result. I had to do things with my family
that I thought were a waste of time when I'd rather be with
my friends. My mom disapproved of my taste in TV shows

(especially *The Love Boat*), and she never did appreciate rock music. I tried to sleep in on Sundays, and sometimes I'd take the thermometer and hold it near my bedside lamp if I didn't want to go to school. I had a rebellious side but a repentant nature. I loved my mom and dad, and I wanted my family's approval. I was a "normal" kid.

To tell you the truth, I have only foggy memories of keeping my diary in seventh grade. I have even foggier memories of the events I recorded, for the most part. But I know as I read through it and as I read the wonderful responses included in this book, written by girls from all over the country . . . 1979, 2007, or the first century A.D. . . . it doesn't matter. I was affected by my world. You are affected by your world. And you know from your early days in Sunday school that even six thousand years ago the world had grown so evil and had influenced so many of *its* inhabitants for evil that God chose to save just one man and his family and start all over again. Read Genesis chapters 6 and 7 if you need a reminder!

It's no worse today. It's just out in the open.

"There will be terrible times in the last days. People will be lovers of themselves, lovers of money, boastful, proud, abusive, disobedient to their parents, ungrateful, unholy, without love, unforgiving, slanderous, without self-control, brutal, not lovers of the good, treacherous, rash, conceited, lovers of pleasure rather than lovers of God—having a form of godliness but denying its power. Have nothing to do with them." 2 Timothy 3:1–5

It's hard to know what to do with "the last days." On the one hand, no one wants to go around being the voice of doom all the time. There is so much to criticize in our world today that it would be easy to become one of those people who go around "painting" everything with a black or grey palette. No color. No hope. And nobody wants to be around someone like that! But there's also a temptation to just join in—eat, drink, and be merry. After all, it's been so long since Jesus went up to heaven; this world doesn't much resemble the world I grew up in, let alone the earth *He* walked upon. The early church didn't have to deal with satellites, the Internet, instant gratification, pornography, Hollywood . . . sometimes it seems like the Bible fails to address the things we have to make decisions about.

Are you living in the last days? Undoubtedly so. But I believe 1979 was "the last days," too. My world and your world—as the song says, it's a small world after all. And perhaps it hasn't changed as much as we think.

## MY STRUGGLE

What parts of your life right now—
entertainment, family, your home, school—
do you think might be important enough to
preserve? How will you remember so that
one day you can tell your grandchildren?

MY ENTERTAINMENT:

MY HOUSE:

MY NEIGHBORHOOD:

MY FAMILY:

MY FRIENDS:


CELL PHONE/IPOD/IM . . . WHAT I CAN'T LIVE WITHOUT:


WHAT I LOVE:


WHAT DISAPPOINTS ME:


MY BIGGEST FEAR:


WHAT I HAVE THE MOST FAITH FOR:

CHAPTER 3

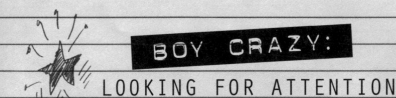

## BOY CRAZY:
## LOOKING FOR ATTENTION

➜ I SAID:

March 26: I like looking at pictures of girls to be married in the newspaper. I figure if they're ugly, so's the guy. But if they're pretty, boy would I like to meet him! I'd like to meet any good looking guy!

August 8: Boy is there a NICE looking guy at the VA. I'm totally in love! He has beautiful blond hair and clear, see through blue eyes. And he likes me! All the girls are crazy about him. Or should I say his looks! Me too! I just can't get that guy off my mind. Boy! Whew. Ahhhh! Fox!!!!!

Day One – The guards in Egypt are cute.

Day Three – That cute waiter smiled at me again.

Day Four – There's a waiter here cuter than the one at the other place. He's a fox!

Day Five – Boy, that waiter is cute.

Day Six – I asked that waiter for a picture. We faced each other and held hands. Our bus driver has awesome eyes. Every day he gets more attractive.

Day Seven: We had to say good-bye to Ali this morning (the waiter). He's married. I would love to be his wife.

Day Eight: A real fox drove our boat on the Sea of Galilee. When I was cold he said, "Stand next to me and you'll be warm." He was even better than Ali. Later that day... Jeff and I took a walk by the ocean and he held my hand. I was scared.

Day Nine: On the top floor of our hotel in Switzerland was a swimming pool. Two naked men walked by. "I liked it!"

Don't worry Mom— your money was well spent on that trip!

## YOU SAID:

I have a boyfriend, so I'm just crazy about one guy. I look for a guy who is on a higher spiritual level than me (or the same). I want a guy who loves God more than he loves me 'cause he can't care about me right if God is not first. I think cussing is the biggest turn-off in the world and if a person is a Christian it is not normally a problem, but I will not date a guy if he cusses 'cause it's my pet peeve. I look for a guy my parents approve of because it's never going to work if they don't like him. I like for my boyfriend to be just as involved in church as I am. I love music and I love it when guys can sing and play guitar.

RACHAEL E., 14

I've never been wild about boys, yeah I've had a couple of crushes and dated a couple of times, but I'm waiting until I'm out of school. I want to finish college before I start looking, but even then, I don't want just a boy. I want a man. I need a guy with a passion for the Lord that at least equals mine, and he has to be able to support himself and a family. I'm very picky, especially when it comes to guys, but I know that God has someone that will meet my every need.

CHANI C., 16

I used to be boy crazy. It was almost all I thought about, boys, boys, boys . . . But then I realized that "boys" were not going to pull me out of sin. "Boys" were not always going to be there when I was sad and lonely. But God was and my Christian family was too. That's when I stopped worshiping Orlando Bloom (someone who didn't know or even want to know me) and started worshiping Jesus Christ (someone who was worth it and who loves me and who died for me). In fact, the guy I marry has to be sort of like that. He's got to love God first. Next he has to care about me, the real me.

BRITTANY R., 14

I wouldn't classify myself as being "boy crazy" but I will admit that I have my moments and that most of the time they don't exactly end up the way I planned for them to. But I'm trying harder to search for true quality rather than settling for the norm. My standards have raised as I've gotten older and looks and social status are no longer more important than personality and spirituality. I want someone who I can talk to about God and who will talk to me about Him too. Someone who appreciates beauty and someone who loves family. I know he's out there waiting and I've got no doubt that God's got it under control.

WHITNEY S.

I'd like to begin this chapter with a shout-out to the girls of this generation. I've taught enough of you in the classroom and have talked to enough of you at retreats and such (and there are two of you living in my home) to know that you have a lot more going on in those brains of yours than I did when I was thirteen. Could I have been any more boy crazy? Was there *anything* going on in my head other than this obsession over boys? Apparently not, or I would have written about those things as well. Instead, my diary reads at times like a tribute to all that is male.

I found my diary only a few years ago. It had been buried along with my childhood stuffed animals, school records, and pictures from my high school plays in my parents' attic for nearly twenty years. I find that the diary reads like a sitcom now, something you'd see on TV Land and laugh really hard because it's so out of date that it's ridiculous. For a while I didn't want to share it with my mom (even as a 35-year-old woman I was hiding my diary from her!) because I was actually ashamed of some of the things I had written.

But the more I read, the more I realized that there was something a lot deeper than crushes going on here. Did you know that the number one need of human beings is to know that they are loved? It's true. When it comes to our physical needs (like food, shelter, and clothes) people can survive, and even be happy, with very little. The same is not true when it comes to our emotional needs. We need to be loved and to know we are loved.

## COULD I HAVE BEEN MORE BOY CRAZY?

May 7: I'm in love again, too! Mike M. And he's single!

May 8: Dan is gonna ask me! I'll say yes!!!

May 9: I was wrong. Dan isn't gonna ask me. He was, but he thinks I'll say no. I didn't really like him a whole lot anyway.

8th Grade — Serious Love:

December 20: I like Jason I.

December 21: I'm going with Doug!

December 28: I was so mad at Doug for not going today that I skated with a bunch of other guys. One was really cute, and he liked me, too.

December 30: I f you want good looking guys, go skiing!

January 1: Two guys yelled at me off the lift.

January 3: My instructor was a total fox!

January 9: I finally broke up with Doug.

January 10: I didn't realize it, but I had a crush on Sam.

January 18: I think about Greg a lot. Like I said, I'm not just looking for A Guy . . . I want GREG!!

*January 19: We had a get together with the old gang from Israel, and even though Jeff wasn't there, I wrote him tonight. It would be great, yet quite a problem, if that letter sparked Jeff's old feelings for me.*

## THE FOLLOWING YEARS . . .

In the years that followed my middle school years, nothing was quite able to deliver me from the madness of my boy-crazy mind. I counted them up in my head, and between my ninth grade year and the year I graduated from college, there were nineteen guys that I was crushing on. Some of these became actual boyfriends, some were crushes from afar, some were good friends who didn't know how much I thought about them . . . but the bottom line is that I never took a vacation. There was always a guy in my fantasies.

I suppose the greatest implication of all this is the sheer number of hours I wasted on nineteen guys that were not going to be my husband. (Not to mention the countless hours I spent ignoring my girlfriends while thinking about those boys.) My college roommates loved me enough to confront me once about this, but I just wasn't ready to hear it.

In Rick Warren's book *The Purpose Driven Life*, he talks about *abiding love*.

> When I first fell in love with my wife,
> I thought of her constantly: while eating
> breakfast, driving to school, attending
> class, waiting in line at the market,
> pumping gas— I could not stop thinking
> about this woman! I often talked to myself
> about her and thought about all the things
> I loved about her. This helped me feel
> close to Kay even though we lived several
> hundred miles apart and attended different
> colleges. By constantly thinking of her,
> I was abiding in her love.[1]

I have to think—good grief! With how many guys have I abided in a *fantasy* love—some of them didn't really even know me and I spent hours imagining conversations, dates, kisses . . . a future that was based on pure fantasy.

And furthermore—abiding so much in the love of a stranger, how much time did I spend during those years getting to know Jesus? How much time was spent abiding in *His* love?

One of my greatest lessons during this time came from my mom just after my graduation from college. We were driving down to Florida to spend a celebratory week together, and I was verbally obsessing over my parting words with my latest crush. I was feeling embarrassed about something I had said to him—I wish it was significant enough that I could tell you now what it was, but I have no idea. After about two hours of this, I guess my mom had had enough.

She looked at me with disbelief and said, "I guess I never realized how egotistical you really are."

"What? How is this egotistical? I'm talking about a relationship—two people—not just about myself."

I'll never forget her next words. "Do you really think you are so important that he's in his apartment right now stewing over what you said? Do you think he's calling his friends to weigh their input in the matter? Suzy, right about now he's thinking, 'What am I going to have for dinner tonight?' You probably don't even figure into the picture at this moment." Had I ever been put in my place!

GODS DIARY

What did I need to know that I was lacking? I needed to know that I had been fearfully and wonderfully made. I needed to know that I was loved with an everlasting love. I needed to know that God had chosen me with my faults and all, and He wanted me to have a relationship with Him that mattered more than anything else in the world . . .

He was probably sad that a relationship with Him was not what I craved the most, but I'm sure that He understood what was happening. After all, it was God Himself who created me and you and all the girls around you to have this natural fascination with the opposite sex. My fascination was natural, right?

Right! But here's the kicker: It's the <u>sin</u> nature that is natural. We are conceived in sin and born in sin, so we can't place too much faith in that which is "natural." I'm not trying to be a downer or overly negative. It's just important to realize that the "normal" feelings and emotions of a teenage girl, or a grown woman for that matter, are not a solid enough foundation for our lives!

As human beings, we are created to be worshipers. And because of this unquenchable drive that God has placed in us . . . we <u>will</u> worship. We do worship. Every living creature has been <u>programmed</u> to give ultimate worth through worship to something. It may be that we worship success and money. Perhaps we worship/idolize a famous actor, musician, or athlete. Some give all their worship to their crush/boyfriend/husband.

Are you interested in putting your acts of worship at the only altar where they truly belong? I know that a lot of you are, and I know that it is <u>not</u> an easy thing to do. But for those of you who are extremely brave . . . here are some pages from God's diary you can meditate on to be sure your attitude toward boys hasn't moved into a form of idolatry.

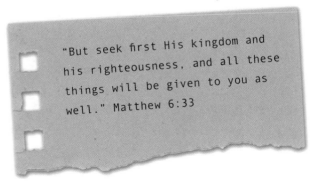

"But seek first His kingdom and his righteousness, and all these things will be given to you as well." Matthew 6:33

This famous verse is planted in the middle of what we call the Sermon on the Mount. At this point in the sermon, Jesus is telling His followers not to get caught up in worry—especially about things like what they wear and what they eat—things that pagans tend to chase after. <u>Instead</u>, He says, <u>chase after Me, because I have every good thing in store for those who seek Me first</u>. So girls . . . step one would be to look at every boy situation in your life, the friends and the crushes, and ask God to show you where it fits in His kingdom. Are you spending a lot of time crushing on a guy while you ignore a girlfriend who really needs you right now? God's kingdom is going to be more about your friend's need. Are you hanging up a lot of posters of hot guys on your bedroom walls and in your locker while spending little or no time loving on God and "hanging out" with Him? God's kingdom always has God alone on the throne of worship.

## MY STRUGGLE

### WHO IS ON THE THRONE?

WHERE DO I SPEND MOST OF MY TIME EACH DAY?

INTERNET_____ MIN. MUSIC _____ MIN.

FRIENDS_____ MIN. SCHOOL _____ MIN.

FAMILY_____ MIN. SPORTS _____ MIN.

GOD_____ MIN. BOYFRIEND _____ MIN.

HOW MUCH OF MY CONVERSATION IS
BASED AROUND . . .

BOYS_____ % SCHOOL_____ %

FRIENDS_____ % SPORTS_____ %

FAMILY_____ % GOD_____ %

I HAVE AT SOME POINT SAID,
"_____ IS MY IDOL!"
(INSERT A PERSON'S NAME)

I CAN HONESTLY SAY THAT I HAVE NO OTHER GODS
THAN MY FATHER IN HEAVEN.

> "You shall have no other gods before me."
>
> EXODUS 20:3

> "Whoever fears God will avoid all extremes."
>
> ECCLESIASTES 7:18B TNIV

This has been one of my favorite guide-verses for years. It's easy to memorize, and it just makes sense to me. Extremes are usually bad news. Verse 16 of this same passage says that extremes can cause you to destroy yourself. Ouch! When a boy enters the picture, examine how much time you are spending thinking of him and talking about him. Ask your girlfriends—do I talk about him too much? They'll be honest with you! Listen to your parents. Are they warning you of an imbalance? Be wise and teachable.

When you have a problem, to whom do you run? A lot of you have written to tell me that

> "The name of the LORD is a strong tower; the righteous run to it and are safe (protected)"
>
> PROVERBS 18:10

your boyfriend understands you like no one else. Other girls, like me once upon a time, will run to guys to fulfill a longing to be noticed. Guys love to rescue girls, and girls love to be rescued, after all. There are two dangers of running to a guy before you run to God. The first is obvious—that guy doesn't love you like God does, and frankly, he doesn't have even a fraction of God's wisdom. He can't save you, and he hasn't promised you every good gift in the heavenly realms. There's just no competition. The second is that there is a tendency for people to get attached to one another when dealing with emotional issues. The more you grow attached to that guy, the more vulnerable you are going to become, and the easier it will be to let physical intimacy come crashing through that door. What starts out as "he understands me" becomes "we've gone too far," and a whole new set of problems is created.

God wants to be first in our lives—whether we are thirteen, twenty, or forty years old, and regardless of our boyfriend status. He comes first. If the guy comes first, he's an idol—we're worshiping him instead of God.

## MY STRUGGLE

Make a list of all the ways you and God have been spending time together lately. It may include prayer, devotions, church, Sunday school, taking long walks, worship music, meeting with a mentor, small groups, a friend with whom you talk about God regularly. Maybe I've left some out. How would you like to increase your "run to God" time?

How we've spent time . . .

 Some new ways to spend time . . .

CHAPTER 4

# GIRLFRIENDS:
## LOOKING FOR ACCEPTANCE

➔ I SAID:

January 31: All of a sudden everyone's best friend is Kim. (Especially boys.) She doesn't drink or smoke or anything, but suddenly she's the in thing. I guess I'm really jealous. I know I am!

March 7: I don't think Kim likes me. She sure doesn't act like it. She likes Ginny, though. After all I did for Cam in art yesterday, she's back to her, "Sue, you're such a dummy," attitude. I knew she was a fake yesterday, as you can see. BIG FAKE!!

May 21: Today had to be the worst day of my life! Just had to be! I really don't like Ginny anymore and frankly I don't care!!! She ignored me all day today and then expected me to be her friend. Well, I'm not gonna! Not ever! Kim and I came close to having a fight, but we stick together. I hope we do forever!

February 7, '80: All the girls said Beth's a ball hog and they're kind of right, but not really. She's very good — and I'm just kind of jealous.

March 22, '80: Beth's so dumb! She and Trish walked way in front of me and Doug at wrestling and Doug took the chance. Practically in the road! I could kill her. I mean I love kissing him, but Beth always sets it up — like I can't myself. Then if I'd do it to her she'd get mad. I might have the main part of Pharoah in the spring play. Beth'd better not get it!

*April 7 '80: There was a big conflict 'cause Steph asked me over and I said yes to her invitation over Beth's invitation. When will she learn I'm not her only pal? (Just her best!)*

## → YOU SAID:

I do get jealous of my friends because they get the guys and the attention that I wanted.

ANGIE R., 13

I've only had a few successful relationships with girls. We always seem to get into fights. Mostly because, and I'll admit it, I like to talk. I sometimes talk to people I shouldn't about things that were supposed to not be said. It gets me into trouble. But I'm not the only one, I've had people do that to me too. I just have a hard time trusting girls as friends.

JENNIFER, 17

My small group at church is five girls who entered high school together and have gone through everything being there for each other. They are my closest group of girlfriends and although we do fight we always are there for each other. We have what I would consider the textbook definition of friendship. I am a bit jealous of the one girl in our group because she is absolutely beautiful and all the boys always notice her. She is such a sweet person, though, so it is hard not to be happy for her.

NICOLE

Guys beat each other up and are done with it. Girls hold grudges. I'm more comfortable in a group of girls, but it's easier to get real relationships with guys.

MEGAN, 15

I definitely have had successful friendships with only a few girls . . . but that is mainly because I like having only a few extremely close friends that you can tell absolutely anything to, rather than a bunch of friends that you do not even know if you can trust.

I definitely have a friend that I feel jealousy toward. One of my friends, Amanda, is extremely pretty . . . blonde, skinny, petite, bright eyes . . . I always feel ugly when I am around her, but she always builds me up, no matter what. ☺

KRYSTLE S., 15

Well to be truthful, I prefer guys, because my best friend . . . I can tell him anything and he won't tell a soul, where if I told a friend of mine that's a girl there would probably be a rumor about me within a half hour.

JESSICA, 14

I have one good friend that I get jealous of sometimes because she makes friends easily and she's a lot more outgoing than I am and a lot of the time I wish I could be like that. There have also been a few times that I've gotten jealous because there have been guys that instantly like her and I felt like I wasn't as good as her because of it.

ANDREA C., 17

There are some guys that are really cool
to hang out with, and I know about one
girl that is a good influence and that I can
trust. But girls are backstabbers, and that is
the way that some of my friends from school
are, and I hate it. It gets on my nerves
because I don't want to tell them anything
and everything, because they might go and
tell everyone.

BLAIR, 12


Guys are so easygoing, and sometimes girls
stress out over really simple things. Like if
I have a problem and I go to a guy for
advice, most of the time they'll give me the
simplest answer to what I thought was a
tough problem.

JESSICA, 15


I would prefer to hang out with boys
because they're not catty like girls are.
When you're with guys, you're actually
having fun. With most girls, you're having fun
at someone else's expense. But, alas, I'm
boy-shy, so I hang out with tomboyish girls.
I have only had a few successful relationships
with girls because I don't talk about other

*people, and a lot of other girls do. I'm
jealous toward all my friends. They seem to
be social butterflies, while I can't even talk
to someone new without panicking.*

*KORTNEE M., 15*

Girlfriends. Can't live with 'em and can't live without 'em, right? Seems like that's a pretty true statement to me! Girls need girls.

There was a time when I would have told you that I prefer the company of guys—no competition. A lot of my reasons were given by girls at the beginning of this chapter: Guys are fun to play games with, they don't constantly criticize what you look like, they aren't constantly giggling or crying, and they don't talk much . . . which means they're not talking about *you* much!

I still enjoy the company of guys, but I have some pretty important relationships with women, too—relationships that I really couldn't do without. My friends are sort of like Baskin Robbins 31 flavors. Boy, do I have an eclectic collection!

I have "girly-girl opposite" friends. They have all of those looks that I would have been totally jealous of in high school. (I'm too mature for that now!) Our friendship works wonderfully, though. They have a lot of qualities that I aspire to—and some that just flat-out leave me scratching my

head because I don't get it. Like long finger-
nails and nail color—I just don't get it!

I have sports buddies. They have
similar passions about sports, competition,
and the outdoors as I do. It's not that we
don't care about clothes or home décor . . .
we love that stuff, too. But our basic
makeup that says sweat is good and even
desirable seems to be pretty harmonious.

I have a mentor. She has all kinds
of wisdom, and an unbelievable passion for
missions. She is an industrious woman (see
Proverbs 31) who is always thinking about
how she can serve others.

I have my daughters—to whom no other
blessings will ever compare! Rachael and
Marie are my day-to-day companions, my
shopping buddies, and my number one test
market. They tell me what clothes look
good, what jokes are funny, and what other
girls will like or dislike. I can trust
them—they are some of my biggest fans, and
I'm definitely their number one fan!

I have Mom—that's my mommy. For years
she's been my bestest girlfriend . . . but

she gets her own chapter. My mother-in-law, Phyllis, has been an amazing gift from God, too. How blessed am I to have TWO godly women who love me, cheer me on, and are loaded with wisdom? (And I used to think they were just loaded with money!)

Why don't you give it a try now? In the next "My Struggle" section, create a list of your own important girl influences. You just may be surprised how many girls are in this thing called life with you.

### GIRLFRIENDS:
### MY OWN CAST OF CHARACTERS

OPPOSITES ATTRACT . . .
girls who make me try new things:

CLONES . . .
girls who are a lot like me:

THE LEGENDS . . .
older girls and women I want to be like:

My mom
My Grandma

MINI MES . . .
younger girls I like hanging with:

Savija

Jaslin

MY SOUL MATES . . .
girls I feel totally at home with:

Gabby

MY CHEERLEADERS . . .
girls who always make me feel better:

Alexis

Gabby

 NOW YOU CREATE A FEW CHARACTERS . . .

MY: Clown is

MY:

MY:

We've just taken some time to consider how much God has blessed us with friends . . . so what in the world happens on such a universal basis that makes most girls prefer hanging out with guys? What has gone so wrong that we make comments like "Girls are mean" or "Girls are backstabbers"? Why do we get so jealous of one another?

Well, ladies, we probably have to start by taking a good, long look in the mirror. When I look in the mirror of 1979, I see a young woman who was pretty desperate to be acknowledged by the other girls as *acceptable*. I wanted to be a sought-after friend. I wanted to be found worthy of their attention and time. And I think I wanted it just as badly as I wanted those same things from the boys. The problem is, my desires were based on a selfish premise: I wanted these things to be given to me, but I didn't feel any need to give them to the other girls. In fact, if the other girls *had* the things I wanted, then those girls were a threat.

As a result, my friends and I went through the maze of junior high and high school like paranoid rats looking for cheese. And when our friends found the cheese first we wished very hard that that cheese might be a little tainted, might make them a little sick . . . or maybe on a good day we'd simply hope that they would share the cheese with us. We didn't know we were doing this; it's simply the way of the selfish heart. When it plays out in our circle of friends, it might look something like this:

Kim is my friend. Dan likes Kim
but I like Dan. Kim becomes a threat.
I no longer like Kim.

Kim ignores me and makes me feel
bad. I get Ginny to ignore Kim with
me. Now Kim is the odd girl out. She
gets a funny look on her face.

My teammate Beth is a good ballplayer.
Good ballplayers get all of the attention.
I want attention. I am mad at Beth.

Steph invites me to her house. Beth
doesn't want me to go. Beth doesn't
want competition for my attention.
Beth is mad at both Steph and me.

It seems pretty silly when it's broken
down into short sequences, doesn't it?

This jealousy of what others have is not unique to girls, and it's not unique to young people. Check out these amazing pictures from the Bible:

Now the serpent was more crafty than any of the wild animals the LORD God had made. He said to the woman, "Did God really say, 'You must not eat from any tree in the garden'?"

The woman said to the serpent, "We may eat fruit from the trees in the garden, but God did say, 'You must not eat fruit from the tree that is in the middle of the garden, and you must not touch it, or you will die.'"

"You will not surely die," the serpent said to the woman. "For God knows that when you eat of it your eyes will be opened, and you will be like God, knowing good and evil." (Genesis 3:1-5)

How many times have you seen this one on a flannel graph:

Now Israel [Jacob] loved Joseph more than any of his other sons, because he had been born to him in his old age; and he made a richly ornamented robe for him. When his brothers saw that their father loved him more than any of them, they hated him and could not speak a kind word to him. (Genesis 37:3-4)

It seeped into Jesus' inner circle of friends:

Then the mother of Zebedee's sons [James and John] came to Jesus with her sons and, kneeling down, asked a favor of him. "What is it you want?" he asked. She said, "Grant that one of these two sons of mine may sit at your right and the other at your left in your kingdom." . . . When the ten heard about this, they were indignant with the two brothers. (Matthew 20:20-21; 24)

And James (Jesus' brother, not the son of Zebedee) gives us this warning:

What causes fights and quarrels among you? Don't they come from your desires that battle within you? You want something but don't get it. You kill and covet, but you cannot have what you want. You quarrel and fight. You do not have, because you do not ask God. When you ask, you do not receive, because you ask with wrong motives, that you may spend what you get on your pleasures. (James 4:1-3)

Have you ever wanted a direct answer from the Bible? It can't get much clearer than that! We fight, girls, because we don't get what we want. We don't get it because we're not asking, and when we do ask we ask with the wrong motives. The Greek word means "terribly," so we're asking "terribly." Satan didn't want to be the only one who was disobedient. This made Adam and Eve a threat. Joseph's brothers wanted their dad's love. This made Joseph a threat. I'm not sure why we are less likely to display this selfishness with our male friends, but I would guess it's simply that they are our opposites. They aren't "competing" for the same thing we are, so they are no threat.

What is threatening you today? What do you covet that the other girls have? There are a few things we could probably do to make our relationships with other girls a little more pleasant, though this disclaimer has to be made first: If you should decide to make some changes in your friendships or the way you relate to other girls, be aware of the fact that they may not immediately change with you. And be prepared to accept the fact that some may never change.

That being said, see what you think of these tactics:

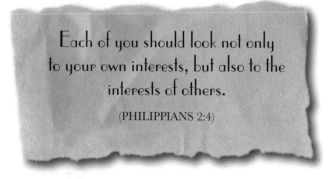

Each of you should look not only to your own interests, but also to the interests of others.

(PHILIPPIANS 2:4)

Okay, I apologize for starting out with such a hard one, but let's get it out of the way, shall we? The girls you know—every one of them—are driven by need. The need to be loved, the need to be accepted, the need to receive mercy—they are the same needs you have. The best way to assure good relationships is to be the first one to say, "You matter more than I do right now." You see, you matter very much to God. What need do you have that He has failed to meet? And what things do you possess that you have somehow gotten through your own power and influence? He's going to take care of you. You don't need to assert your needs 24/7. Remember from the last chapter . . . the pagans run after things like that, and your heavenly Father knows what you need (Matthew 6:32). So the guy you like seems to think your friend is more his style. Can you say, "Hey, she's important, too. God has my back. My turn is coming." Maybe she's a better musician than you—she keeps beating you out for first chair in orchestra, or everyone's always talking about her sweet guitar skills. Doesn't she have the need for encouragement and praise just like you do? I guess another way to say it is . . . get over it! It's not all about you.

> Confess your sins to each other and pray for each other so that you may be healed. The prayer of a righteous person is powerful and effective. (James 5:16 TNIV)

Prayer should be as much a part of our day as breathing. God's Word says we are to pray continually, pray on all occasions, pray with thanksgiving, pray for one another, pray for those who mistreat you, pray that you will not fall into temptation. He hears us when we pray, He comes near when we pray, and this verse adds another bonus of prayer . . . He heals us when we pray. But why do we need to confess our sins to each other before prayer?

Not too long ago my husband and I tried a "life-style diet" where we did not eat processed (junk) food, but focused on natural things like fruit and vegetables, as well as smaller portions. On the first night of the diet, I stayed up later than he did, and as soon as I heard him snoring upstairs, I quietly went to the cupboard and ate a cinnamon Pop-Tart. I cheated. If I had confessed this to him (and I stand guilty of not confessing it, until he reads this, of course), what are the chances I would have eaten another Pop-Tart the next night? He would know to ask me . . . Did you cheat on your diet again last night? Hidden sin is easy sin. I can eat all the Pop-Tarts I want as long as I am the only one who knows . . um, except for God. If you tell someone that you are struggling with jealousy or bitterness toward someone, it'll be a lot harder for you to hold on to it. Your friendships will be on their way to healing.

> The son of man did not come to
> be served, but to serve, and to
> give his life as a ransom for many.
>
> (MATTHEW 20:28)

Ultimately, you have a decision to make. Do you want to spend the rest of your life expecting to be served, or will you make the very unusual choice to be a servant? Here's a radical idea—what if we replaced that mental list of all the things that "stink" in our lives with an actual, physical list of things we could do to bless other people? There'd be very little time for pity parties! And those girls who seem to be threats now . . . they'd be little blessings just waiting to happen. It might seem a little too much like Leave It to Beaver or The Brady Bunch . . . but why did we ever let our world tell us that kindness and truth are totally out of fashion?

As long as we're seeking our own interests, ladies, we're not going to be able to get along with one another. We're just too much alike, and we'll all be chasing after the same thing. And then we're going to see each other as the competition—even our best friends will be threats. The only way we can all chase the same thing is if that thing we all chase is . . . you guessed it . . . the kingdom of God.

## MY STRUGGLE

What are some things you've been jealous of in your friends' lives or have been in competition over? What will it take for you to surrender those things?

DELIVER ME, O JESUS,

From the desire of being loved,
From the desire of being extolled,
From the desire of being honored,
From the desire of being praised,
From the desire of being preferred,
From the desire of being consulted,
From the desire of being approved,
From the desire of being popular,
From the fear of being humiliated,
From the fear of being despised,
From the fear of suffering rebuke,
From the fear of being *calumniated,
From the fear of being forgotten,
From the fear of being wronged,
From the fear of being ridiculed,
From the fear of being suspected,
Amen.[1]

(*Lied about)

CHAPTER 5

➤ I SAID:

March 13: It should have been good (today) because we went rollerskating. But I had a rotten time. You'd think that with three single, good-looking guys there, one would ask me to skate. Oh, but no, Sue's too ugly to even be seen with. And I don't usually fall. Well, I went on my can three times. I was trying to show off. And school was even worse. What a drag.

➤ March 14: Ellen F. really knows how to charm people. Today she told me I was too white. Everyone said, "(Gosh) Ellen, you're real nice." I didn't care. I'm used to being put down.

March 15: I really don't know where to begin. There is one thing I really wanted to yell at myself for yesterday, and that's being too conceited. In gym I always find myself saying to myself, "Boys, they stink. I'm great. No one is better than me. Watch me show up Miss S." I just wanted to mention that 'cause it upsets me.

December 20: ▓▓▓ I like Jason L., but I'm pretty sure he doesn't like me. If I were in 7th grade I'd feel pretty dumb goin' with an 8th grader, too. But it's really 'cause I'm ugly that he doesn't like me!

February 22, '80: I felt really weird today. I know I act kind of crazy and I'm trying to quit, but it's hard. I think that's what guys don't like about me. But Beth's crazy, too, and look at her. I'm not gorgeous.

March 18, '80: We did our Muppet show again and it came out really good. Better than Sunday. They took pictures for the yearbook, too. Bet I look ugly.

May 27, '80: I'm not Valedictorian or Salutatorian — but I'm only $1/100^{th}$ away. No one could believe it! What a close race! I'll tell ya, it feels awful to be the loser. I feel like a scum and the teachers are acting weird around me. Maybe it's just me.

*June 28, '80: The day ended up pretty good, but like always I felt ugly, fat, and very un-beautiful.*

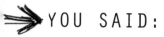

> YOU SAID:

Sometimes it is hard to keep on saying I am beautiful when there are so many other prettier people in magazines and at school and when people say you have to look a certain way just to get a boyfriend. But I realized that the truth is everybody feels that way at school. And the other truth is, is that the people in the magazines don't really look like that. That's what hair and make-up teams are for. Everybody is beautiful in God's eyes and it doesn't matter what other people say.

ARIANA, 11

It's almost like a little dictator lives in my head and shouts horrible things at me if I look in the mirror and like what I see.

BRITAINEY, 18

I do not consider myself beautiful. It's hard to explain, when I look in the mirror I see this horrid image, but I know that I am beautiful. I know that what I see is not me, because I know God cannot make a horrid thing. I only wish I could see the beauty everyone else sees. It is so sad.

BRANDI

At times I consider myself beautiful. But most of the time I have trouble getting myself to believe that because a lot of school peers have told me otherwise in previous years and it took a huge toll on my self-esteem.

JORDAN W., 14

This is actually a hard subject to discuss with me. I guess I don't personally feel beautiful. My friends have always told me that I should be a model and that I am, "Oh, so pretty!" I guess the whole reason I don't believe I am beautiful is because I don't want others to think I am vain at all. I want to be humble about it and just ignore the comments. But when I start to ignore the comments is when the devil is at his prime attacking me every time I look in the mirror. I believe that this is one of the areas in my life that God and I need to discuss more, because the devil knows this is one of my biggest weaknesses and he will do anything to break me.

KAITLYN, 17

For the longest time I did not consider myself beautiful. I had many negative thoughts and low self-esteem. I got made fun of and picked on quite often by my peers. It hurt me so much. To this day I still struggle with bad acne. It can be really humiliating at times. But through it all I was able to get past that. In the end it drew me closer to God and I realized then that it's not what's on the outside that matters. It's what's on the inside that counts. God sees into my heart and knows I'm beautiful. He created me in His very own image.

NICOLE B., 17

*I think I am beautiful. Any struggles I've had I believe made me even more so. My personality is unmatchable. My looks are whatever they are. I struggled with various eating disorders for 5 years. I was a binger, purger, non-eater, pill-eater, lalala. Learned my lesson after being in the hospital so many times. Not worth your temperature being 92 degrees and your heart barely beating.*

*JESSICA, 16*

Okay, girls, what's up? Self-loathing must be one of Satan's chief troublemakers,'cause I'll tell you, he's got quite a grip on us here! It's simply unreal how many of us are struggling from day to day with the *idea* of beauty and issues of self-esteem.

Let's tackle beauty first. In the paragraph above this one you'll notice I called beauty an "idea" . . . it's not a real, concrete thing. It's what we call in the English business an *abstract noun*. If this were *Schoolhouse Rock*, I might be reminding you right now that a noun can be a person, place, thing, or *idea*.

There is a picture of beauty that each of us has accepted and planted firmly in our minds. There is an anonymous quote (sometimes credited to Plato, as opposed to Disney's Pluto who never says anything): "Beauty is in the eye of the beholder." Unfortunately—and I'm sure this will be no shock to you—many of us have accepted an idea of beauty that has been created by magazines and professional photographers with unbelievable airbrushing skills. Have you ever seen a professional model or a movie star as they roll out of bed in the morning? You probably haven't, but tomorrow when you wake up, go look in the mirror. Note the bed head, the pillow creases in your face, the new pimples that have popped up, the dry skin, the teeth that need to be brushed and the puffy eyes . . . That's exactly what a model sees when she rolls out of bed! And imagine what you might look like if you had a personal trainer, an agent, a dietician, a makeup artist and personal stylist waiting for you before school each morning. Of course you'd have to wake up at about 4 a.m. each day, because looking that good takes a long time, but just imagine!

One of my favorite stories about retouching the famous bod comes from a February 2003 cover shot of actress Kate Winslet for Britain's *GQ* magazine. Apparently Kate's legs were messed with pretty good on that magazine cover. The actress did give permission for digital touch-ups to be done, but not to the extent the magazine eventually went.

> "The retouching is excessive. I do not look like that and more importantly I don't desire to look like that. I actually have a Polaroid that the photographer gave me on the day of the shoot . . . I can tell you they've reduced the size of my legs by about a third. For my money it looks pretty good the way it was taken."[1]

And Kate isn't the only one who's gotten worked up over retouched photos. Also in 2003, *Redbook* was in trouble with both its June and July cover photo—neither of which was real! On *Redbook*'s July cover, Julia Roberts's head came from a paparazzi shot taken at the 2002 People's Choice awards. Her body, however, was from her *Notting Hill* movie premiere four years earlier. The photo was described by *USA Today* as "bizarre at best and freakish at worst."

One month earlier, Jennifer Aniston had refused to give *Redbook* a photoshoot because she was already committed to another magazine for a cover photo. *Redbook* informed Aniston's manager that she would appear on their cover anyhow. The resulting photo was mismatched, according to Aniston, and came from *three* separate photos. The magazine denied the charges, saying they had manipulated only her shirt color and the length of her hair.

In May 2003, *Seventeen* magazine had to send an apology and a "gift" to Sarah Michelle Gellar after changing her shirt color and making her left hand appear "unnaturally long and misshapen." [2]

These are not isolated occurrences. According to *GQ* editor Dylan Jones, "Almost no picture that appears in *GQ* . . . has not been digitally altered in some way." His explanation of what the magazine did to Winslet was as follows: "Various parts have been improved, including her stomach and legs," said Jones. [3]

Excuse me? Improved? You see, when we measure value, worth, and esteem by this world's standards of beauty, we run into trouble. We begin to sense need for "improvement," even after we are commanding fifteen million dollars for every motion picture we make. After all, there's always someone who is more beautiful, and what is beautiful today may be totally out tomorrow. You may think as I do—if Kate Winslet needed improvement, what does that say about ME?

Or how about these Christian taboo words: Self-Esteem. I can remember a time when a Christian didn't dare talk about having self-esteem or, worse yet, loving herself.

On the whole I have to admit that I understand the threat of these words. They seem to fly in the face of some pretty basic biblical truths, such as:

## WHAT IF IT'S TRUE?

Beauty is in the eye of the beholder, and it may be necessary from time to time to give a stupid or misinformed beholder a black eye.

MISS PIGGY

Rarely do great beauty and great virtue dwell together.

PETRARCH (ITALIAN POET AND SCHOLAR IN THE 1300S)

"Whoever exalts himself will be humbled, and whoever humbles himself will be exalted."
Matthew 23:12

"It is not good to eat too much honey, nor is it honorable to seek one's own honor."
Proverbs 25:27

After all, these are the things that tripped up Satan in the garden, right? Satan wanted to be like God—he wanted to be the greatest. And that scares me, because I know that all throughout my life I've struggled with wanting to be the greatest. My mom says that when I was a very little girl, I had to have as much to eat as my brothers. I never finished it all, but I had to put everything on my plate they had put on theirs.

Even now when I golf with my husband I have to hit off the men's tees. If I beat him off the women's tees, I can't just say, "I won." There's a qualification—yeah, you won, but your tees were closer to the hole. It's a running joke in our family—he always makes that excuse if I beat him; but the truth is *I* have to know I beat him off the same tees he hit from.

So I've struggled with some of the same things as Satan . . . How scary is that?! Even though God has covered me with the blood of Jesus Christ, and that's all God sees when He looks at me, I know the truth. Apart from Him, I am a mess! Without that covering I'm soiled, stained . . . like someone who is seriously challenged for common sense has just carpeted their toddler's toy room with white carpet and then installed a juice bar that serves only grape juice with no sippy cups. Get the idea? But the point remains . . . what does *God* see when He looks at me? He has given me the right to be called a child of God. He has redeemed me. He redeemed me because of *His* great love, not because I'm deserving, but hey—I still stand redeemed.

GOD'S DIARY

Look at all of the amazing things God says about us in Psalm 139 alone:

He has laid His hand on us. (verse 5)

There is no way we can escape His presence. (verse 7)

His right hand holds us fast. (verse 10)

He knit us together in our mothers' wombs. (verse 13)

We are fearfully and wonderfully made. (verse 14)

All the days ordained for us were written in His book before even one of them came to be. (verse 16)

I won't bore you too much with science—besides, I stink at science—but have you ever studied something called genetics? Genetics is a science of probability, based on DNA, which determines a lot about our physical and even emotional makeup. Genes determine whether we will be tall or short, have straight or curly hair, whether a guy will keep his hair as he gets older or be really foxy and baldish like my husband, and even whether we will be stimulated by people (extrovert) or exhausted by them (introvert). It's a pretty interesting science, and it's good science.

But it's really bad theology. You are not a product of chance. No matter how many sperm were released at your conception (between 300 and 500 million!!!), only ONE of those sperm had any chance of creating you. ("All the days ordained for me were written in your book before one of them came to be." "You knit me together in my mother's womb.") Of the millions of sperm released, only a few hundred actually survived long enough to confront the egg. At least two hundred sperm pushed relentlessly against the egg's tough outer membrane until the membrane was weakened enough to allow ONE sperm to penetrate the egg.

Then, according to the UK Web site Baby Centre: "The gender of baby depends on which type of sperm burrows into the egg first—sperm with a Y chromosome will make a boy baby, and sperm with an X chromosome will make a girl. There are plenty of myths about how to conceive a boy or girl, and some are backed by a bit of scientific evidence, but on the whole, a child's sex is determined randomly."[4]

Really? Do you think there is any probability that God left control over that one victorious sperm to chance? You may, like me at times, struggle with the idea that you cannot possibly exist apart from some cosmic mistake—honestly, sometimes I feel like I am just one big "E is for Error" on the score sheet of life—but when I consider the God I know and have a relationship with, I see the truth.

God is tickled silly pink, madly in love with you. He sees you. He knows all of your insecurities, all of the things you consider flaws and weaknesses. He knows of your rebellion—your inability to do the good things you want to do and your tendency to do the opposite instead. He knows what other people think of you and what they say about you—and what you think and say of others. And He loves you regardless. He covers you with His tenderness because you are His beautiful princess. He sings a song of redemption and pure love over you . . . at least that's what He desires to do. He says it Himself: "The LORD your God is with you, he is mighty to save. He will take great delight in you, he will quiet you with his love, he will rejoice over you with singing" (Zephaniah 3:17).

And here's the kicker with this whole issue of self-esteem. Once we realize who we are in Christ, our relationships with others take on a totally new dimension. We realize that anyone who knows these things about God—that He created them, that He loves them, that He has planned a relationship with them from the beginning—walks in freedom. And anyone who doesn't know these things about God . . . well, they sort of have trouble relating to other people. They play power games. They gossip, argue, and struggle. Sometimes they are just plain mean. But once we know who we are, we can see through that in others, and it leaves us feeling compassionate instead of combative.

Bottom line . . . Once we truly know that we are loved, that we matter more than life itself, we can truly rejoice at the amazing things God has done in other girls' lives without feeling the slightest twinge of envy, competition, or inferiority.

# MY STRUGGLE

Make a list below of all the things you really dislike about yourself. Be thorough. Maybe even get online and ask a couple of friends, "Hey, what do I complain about (about myself) all the time?"

Now read Psalm 139. Write down your favorite snippet from this psalm. Put it on an index card or a nice note card and hang it on your primary mirror—the one you use to get ready each morning.

MY FAVORITE PART OF PSALM 139:

CHAPTER 6

## MEAN GIRLS:
### LOOKING FOR POWER

→ I SAID:

March 16: You know, it's a terrible feeling to hurt someone's feelings. I wrote Sam W. notes all day and I really had him going. I mean he really liked me. Then I had to tell him it was a joke and he took it pretty hard. I calmed him down though and now we're friends.

April 20: Kim made a good one today. I gave her a compass and told her to poke Polly in the butt with it. Kim just said, "No, it might pop." We all cracked up and Ginny got in trouble for laughing too loud.

May 19: I believe and trust in God, and may I be forgiven

for saying this, but the family we stayed with were all fat dweebs except for the mom and the little boy. He was really cute, and the mom just sat there and watched t.v. I really got into it when she didn't make a big fuss over the fact that I just got back from the Holy Lands. The dweeby man bored me with his stupid questions.

February 8: Well, it's final. Kim is no longer my friend. At school today she would whisper in front of me and when I asked her what she said, she said, "Nothing," and her and Tara laughed. Steph and I are just ignoring her. I gave Steph a life saver and Kim got a real weird look on her face 'cause I didn't give her one.

March 9: Kim is getting worse all the time. Today she was talking to Jara and when I walked up she said, "Get out of here, we're talking." I don't know what she's trying to prove. She's no one special and someone ought to drill that ~~xxxx~~ fact into her. Maybe I should. I'm beginning to hate her.

 YOU SAID:

I'm homeschooled so I'm kinda sheltered now but when I was in public school, heck yes! There were tons of mean girls, some who were mean by cussing at you, some who physically hurt you, and some who emotionally hurt you by acting like your friend and saying things about you that aren't true behind your back. But I've come to terms with it and I've realized that they were just jealous somehow.

JESSICA, 15

My relationships since 7th grade have changed
a lot . . . I never had friends in the 7th
grade; I was the gothic outcast . . . and not
that they didn't like me. They were scared of
me because I dressed all in black and wore
a trench coat . . . My freshman year I
had a whole bunch of friends telling me the
reason they would never talk to me or sit by
me in 7th grade was not that they hated me,
but they were scared of me . . . it made me
realize I was never really hated.

BRANDI, 17

In 5th grade I was in the "popular group."
I always seemed to be different than them.
They always picked on me, so one day I
just left them. I went to go hang out with
Amanda (my best friend now). I have been
so much happier since I left them 'cause I
don't have to worry about losing friends
'cause of what I wear. Sure I still care about
what I wear, but now I can pick what I want
to wear. I don't follow what other people
wear. I make up stuff and some people
follow me. That's a good feeling. I have

never tried to be mean just to fit in. I like to stick out in a crowd, but not like that.

AMBER, 13

Everyone starts out in elementary school at the same level, then once they hit about 7th grade and high school we start to learn about a great thing called cliques. Everyone splits off and we all become judged by each other. I have never been in the popular crowd and probably never will be. I actually am pretty proud of that because I would never have to worry about trying to fit in.

KAITLYN, 17

In elementary the mean girls got to me a lot! But that's when I was so boyish. It's weird I got out of that stage when I became a Christian and that's when I became the mean girl! I would pick on girls I knew were just like me; they were the easiest to pick on. I'm not going to lie—it was fun, but once I got to the 11th grade it was not fun and I saw how rude it was. God really had to move in me. I regret what I did and I wished that I didn't get caught up in it.

JULIE B., 18

I don't think there's a girl in the universe that hasn't been cut down by another girl. I don't think there's a girl in the universe that feels like everyone loves her, and I don't think there's a girl in the universe that can honestly say she doesn't care what a single person thinks about her. When push comes to shove, insults hurt and everyone cries at some point or another. That's where I come in, and that's why I'm out of that whole "popularity feature." I hang out with just about anyone. Geeks, Freaks, Jocks, Punks, Goths . . . just about anyone who cares enough to come down and talk. I don't really think I've ever been seriously popular . . . or popular at all for that matter. I'm not like everyone else, and that's the beauty in it.

TAYLOR ANNE, 13

➤ Mean Girls. Have you seen the movie? New girl Cadi (Lindsay Lohan) moves to Evanston, Illinois, after being homeschooled for fifteen years by her wildlife research parents in Africa. She's had amazing adventures all her life, but knows nothing of America and how American high schools work. She ends up, of course, in a completely satirized version of the average American school—meaning it's more of a cartoonlike picture than a real one. I doubt your teachers are as incompetent and reckless as Cadi's teachers. The first time we meet Cadi's math teacher (ex-*Saturday Night Live* actress Tina Fey) she has had her coffee spilled all down her front, so she of course has to remove her sweater . . . in front of the entire class and her boss . . . and of course her undershirt comes up, too . . . and of course not one kid in the class seems too concerned. I don't know about you, but if that had happened in one of my classes, I think a few kids would have fainted, some would have screamed, most would have covered their faces, maybe one or two would laugh . . . or vomit.

The point is, you know from the beginning that Cadi's problems with the other girls are going to be huge. Backbiting, gossip, sabotage, isolation, lying, trickery . . . but wait a minute! *That* doesn't sound exaggerated. *That's* not so cartoonlike. That's like my school . . . and yours.

If you want a great description of what we girls do to one another, there is one excellent read I can recommend. *Queen Bees and Wannabes*[1] is actually the inspiration for the movie *Mean Girls*. Author Rosalind Wiseman paints a clear picture of what we girls do to one another. When boys bully, they do so by physical intimidation. They push one another around and draw blood whenever possible. Then it's over. It's forgotten. But being bullied by a girl is far worse.

Girls have learned the fine art of isolation. When we become threatened by another girl, for any reason—maybe she likes the same guy I do; maybe I can't understand the way she dresses, walks, or talks; maybe she has potential to be more popular than I am—we take out the most effective feminine weapon in existence. We tell all of the other girls not to talk to her. We purposefully do not invite her to a party, and if that weren't enough, we let everyone know to spread the word that she is not invited. We whisper in front of her. We tell her where she can sit and where she can't. And, oh, the "looks"! Do we ever have the entire collection of "looks" down?

I think I know why we girls do this to one another—it's just a theory, just a hunch, but I think I have this figured out. It goes back to chapter 3 where we were talking about our primary need is that of being loved. For some reason, when we leave the security of childhood, it's not enough to know that God loves us, that our parents are crazy about us, and that we have one or two really good friends who would never let us down . . . We develop instead this insatiable need to be popular. We have to be appreciated. We have to be noticed and talked about, and sometimes it's even okay with us if the talk about us isn't good talk. We just need to be talked about.

This change doesn't happen to everyone. Somehow a few of us manage to stay stable and levelheaded, not falling prey to popularity and gossip and "he said, she said." Some of us befriend a wide range of people and stay relatively happy through it all. But this percentage of unaffected girls is extremely low.

I was one of these "unaffected" girls through most of my school years, but 7th and 8th grade did not leave me unscarred. And most of you did not make it through this maze safely either. At some point you were likely one of four girls:

## THE MEAN GIRL

You may have been (or perhaps you are now) the meanest of all girls. You are a leader in your group. Other girls will follow your lead to say mean things about your "friends," or to ignore them if need be. It may be understood by the other girls that you get first pick when it comes to guys, even if the guy you want happens to be dating someone else. And woe to the girl who gets in your way—you have a lot of other girls behind you who will go to war for you if anyone is foolish enough to cross you.

Why do you do this? I think mean girls are the most desperate to be loved, and the most unaware that they are love-*able*. They may give off an air of "I'm all that" . . . but the truth is they are terrified that they are *NOT* all that. They fear being normal or average in the eyes of their peers, because normal carries no power, and power can feel like a good substitute for love.

But power without love is empty. First Corinthians 13 is a chapter you've often heard read at weddings, but when written it wasn't really intended to be "the wedding verse." It was written to a church in a place called Corinth—a church, oddly enough, that was having some troubles getting along with one another.

If I speak in the tongues of men and of angels, but have not love, I am only a resounding gong or a clanging cymbal. If I have the gift of prophecy and can fathom all mysteries and all knowledge, and if I have a faith that can move mountains, but have not love, I am nothing. If I give all I possess to the poor and surrender my body to the flames, but have not love, I gain nothing.

That would be verses 1 through 3. You are familiar with the rest, where the qualities of love are listed so plainly.

| LOVE IS . . . | LOVE IS NOT . . . |
|---|---|
| • Patient | • Envious |
| • Kind | • Boastful |
| • Truthful | • Prideful |
| • Protective | • Rude |
| • Trusting | • Selfish |
| • Hopeful | • Angry |
| • Long-lasting | • Keeping a record of past wrongs |
| | • Happy with evil |

You probably don't need me or anyone else to tell you at this point whether you are a mean girl! Love is not rocket science. You either operate out of love, the stuff on the left side of the chart above, and everyone can see that . . . or you operate out of envy, jealousy, and pride . . . and everyone can see that, too.

## THE SIDEKICK

You could also be one of those feisty sidekick girls, ready to stand up for the most popular girl no matter what. You are secretly jealous of her social position, but being her friend and confidante is much better than the alternative—being her target. You may or may not actually like the mean girl, but you know that you don't dare get on her bad side; at any moment she could turn the other girls on you. So rather than challenge the way things are, you go along with whatever the mean girl says.

This leaves you feeling sad, confused, and frightened a lot of the time, but rarely do you feel settled and at peace. You have probably "had to" say things you didn't really mean and hurt people you didn't want to hurt. You may find yourself saying one thing to one group of friends and then turning around and saying the exact opposite to someone else. I know this because I've been there! I think a couple of times I even lied to my parents and teachers in order to protect the mean girl or my position in the popular group . . . to me that felt the worst of all.

The funny thing is, I felt like I really had everyone fooled. I was a great student in middle school—I worked in my school's version of "accelerated classes" and was in a three-way tie for middle school valedictorian. I thought that my grades and the way I "sucked up" to my teachers would amount to being considered a leader in their eyes . . . but listen to this entry from my 1979 diary:

School is out! Boy ~~it~~ it's about time. School is going to be great next year. No more Gena, no more Jara; boy what a blast. I'm not ~~sorry~~ I called Gina a (bleep), 'cause she is one. I hate her and so do many other people. May she die!! And the same goes for Jessica!

And from the same day—the *very same* day:

> It was really boring all day long and the best part was chapel. It was fun to sing with the choir again. Real fun. In a way I'm sorry that I didn't make the Student Life Committee. I love God more than anything, no matter how much I get in trouble. I LOVE GOD!!! ♥

When I'm out talking to girls and read that particular journal entry, there are always two predictable reactions. The first is that you can hear a very loud *GASP* when I read, "May she die!!" The second is that the girls *laugh* when I read, "I love God more than anything . . ."

They laugh. Is it *funny?* No, but girls recognize immediately that I was the poster child for hypocrisy in that journal entry. I said two completely contrasting things. And you know, there's a certain Bible verse that I was a poster child for on June 6, 1979, too.

> With the tongue we praise our Lord and
> Father, and with it we curse human beings,
> who have been made in God's likeness. Out of
> the same mouth come praise and cursing. My
> brothers and sisters, this should not be. Can
> both fresh water and salt water flow from
> the same spring? My brothers and sisters,
> can a fig tree bear olives or a grapevine
> bear figs? Neither can a salt spring produce
> fresh water. (James 3:9-12 TNIV)

But you see, the mean girl and the girl who plays the sidekick—who willingly gets caught in the middle—just might be *posers*. I use that word because I know it is *not* a good word these days. Nobody wants to be called a poser; it's all about keeping it real. And I have to agree that real is good. But which is it? Are you a fig tree, using your tongue to praise God and encourage the people who have been made in God's image . . . By the way, that would include *all* the girls in your school and in your church. Or are you another type of tree, using your mouth for curses and bitterness? Because, you see, you can't be both.

My teachers were aware that I couldn't possibly be both. I remember the day that the Student Life Committee was announced. I had really hoped to be chosen. It was to be a group of students who met with the teachers, who counseled their peers, and who made decisions on behalf of the student body—a kind of student council. Being a member of the SLC suggested that you were a leader who had the respect of both the student body, which nominated you, and your teachers, who approved you. I was angry that I hadn't been chosen! Look at my grades, for crying out loud! And I was popular! It ticked me off, and I remember seething about being overlooked, complaining to my friends, casting "looks" at teachers . . .

Wow. Did they ever nail my character to a T. I was not SLC material. Are you? Would your teachers say that they see character and integrity in your life? Could you be trusted to counsel your peers, or have you smeared too many of them to do a job like that with any kind of honesty? Are you under the impression that both fresh- and saltwater can pour out of your mouth? Because that's impossible. You're one thing or you're another. I was not freshwater, no matter how hard I tried to fool my teachers and my friends.

## THE TARGET

Sadly, you may be the target of the mean girl and her group. No matter what you do it is not good enough; in fact, you seem to do better when you *ignore* the existence of the popular girls altogether. Any attempts on your behalf to

"You don't have to listen to those mean girls. They're just there to make you upset and make you feel bad about yourself. And you know, really, inside, they feel bad about themselves, too, but they won't admit it to anybody." (Karen from Mean Girls.)

befriend group members seem to backfire and only provide more fuel for their cruel fire.

Well, I have good news and bad news for you. The good news is that by tenth grade or so, despite what *Mean Girls* may have portrayed, the truly cruel girls have very little power over anyone any longer—unless you choose to let them bother you, they probably won't. Even most of the boys will have lost considerable patience with them—in a way, they begin to write out an order for their own extinction. Oh, they'll still parade about the school with some importance they have given to themselves, but very few people will be impressed with them any longer.

The bad news is . . . when you are in the midst of being a target, there's very little you can *do* to change the situation other than ride it out. If you are being physically harmed or threatened you need to tell your parents and your teachers. If the attacks are just verbal, I *still* suggest you let your parents and teachers in on it; even if you don't want them to do anything about it there is a lot of good that can come from them knowing what's going on. First of all, they can keep an eye on things and maybe catch the harassment red-handed. Then it doesn't look like you've ratted on anyone, but the girls who are hurting you can be confronted by authority. Secondly, your teachers, parents, and youth leaders may have had an experience like yours when they were younger, and wouldn't it just feel good to know that you're not alone? Maybe they have good advice to give you. Maybe you'd just like to get a big old hug from them and be reminded once again that you are tremendously loved.

The bottom line is—if you don't tell anyone what you're going through, you suffer alone. And if you suffer alone you may be able to convince yourself that you deserve it, that no one understands, that no one cares, or that you are an undeserving victim . . . and all of those are mind-sets that Satan would love for you to have, because they are all hurtful and destructive. And in most cases, they are all lies to boot.

## Living in Comfort

The final category you may fit into is that of the girl who is generally well adjusted and has a lot of friends across the entire spectrum of cliques at school—band people, jocks, preps, the mathletes . . . you like them all. Nearly half of you will fall into this category—it's not at all unusual.

You are the girl who enjoys school, probably both for its academic and social aspects. You have plenty of friends and adjust easily to whichever group you happen to be with. You see the mean girls in action and it makes you feel a bit indignant with the mean girl while feeling compassion for the target. Here's the deal with this group, though: Jesus never called us to be comfortable! Though you are kind and peace-loving, though there is very little drama in your life, comfort can be for some a road that leads only to apathy. It's a nice road with a very pretty view and a lot of nifty shops to stop at along the way, but it is ultimately a dead-end street.

My daughters have recently had to go through the ordeal of being "the new girl" both at school and church. While my youngest suffered a little at the hands of mean girls, my oldest was more a victim of comfort. Think about it . . . you have a group of friends, right? You are comfortable with one another and enjoy doing things together (probably why you became friends in the first place). When someone new comes along it takes a lot of effort to be inclusive. They don't know any of the inside jokes, they weren't there on that one day last year that the rest of you had the best time of your lives—in fact, one major component of friendship is missing: memories. Since my Rachael's memories were all the way across the country in Santa Barbara . . . she was often left out when the other girls would get together.

So we find it easiest to stay with those we know the best. It's comfortable. In the meantime, however, the other 50 percent of the feminine world is waiting for a hero! What might happen if, instead of sitting at your table of regulars for lunch tomorrow, you went out on a limb and sat with that girl you have noticed *always* sits alone? What might happen if you (and maybe a couple of others, if this is too intimidating) approached the scene of a crime (a single girl being targeted by mean girls) and physically rescued the target from the grips of her predators? What might happen? You might become a target? I suppose so. But you may also make a friend. And, like I did so many years ago, you may become the poster child for a Bible verse or two . . . only *you* may do so in a very positive manner.

GOD'S DIARY

Try these verses on for size:

"And as for you, brothers and sisters, never tire of doing what is good."
2 Thessalonians 3:13 TNIV

"In the same way, let your light shine before men, that they may see your good deeds and praise your Father in heaven." Matthew 5:16

"Speak up for those who cannot speak for themselves, for the rights of all who are destitute. Speak up and judge fairly; defend the rights of the poor and needy." Proverbs 31:8-9

You know, it can't get much clearer than that. Nearly every directive that God gives us in His Word revolves around two things: worshiping Him and loving our neighbor. And, I might point out to the comfortable . . . they all include verbs of action. Girls, it's time to rise up and start an absolute revolution. A revolution is an uprising that causes, according to my dictionary, complete change. Do you want to be a revolutionary? I guarantee there are a lot of girls who will follow you if you are bold enough to get it started.

## DID YOU KNOW?

The words "tire of" in 2 Thessalonians 3:13 come from the Greek enkakeo, and literally mean "to become exasperated by difficulty." I don't know about you, but in my book of logic that means when I try to do good I will experience difficulty!

## MY STRUGGLE

Which of the four groups did you find yourself in?

- MEAN GIRL
- TARGET
- SIDEKICK
- COMFORTABLE

### HERE'S YOUR REVOLUTIONARY COURSE OF ACTION:

#### MEAN GIRLS AND SIDEKICKS

First, take some time to pray. Read the section in the following chapter entitled "Revolution." Your revolutionary task is to make a list of girls you have targeted . . . and to seek forgiveness. There are several ways this can be done. You can be bolder than bold and just straight up ask for it. "Hey, I know I've been pretty nasty to you, but some things have changed lately for me and I was just wondering if you could forgive me." You could also make things right by simply changing your behavior. End relationships with mean girls who don't want to change and begin giving your targets a chance to be part of your life. Smile at them, talk to them, or sit with them at lunch. Either way, expect to lose a few friends who do not share your conviction that the mean days need to come to an end!

#### TARGETS

You probably have every "right" to be angry and bitter. After all, you've done nothing to invite other girls to treat you this way. You may have even gone out of your way to be kind. Part of following Jesus means surrendering our "rights." Jesus did that when He went to the cross for us . . . and then He tells us, "If anyone wants to follow Me he must first take up his own cross." Bitterness and anger do not bring healing to anyone, especially to the one who is holding on to the anger. Your revolutionary task is to first of all forgive. Tell God that you need His help (because you do!!!), and then take it a day at a time. You may need to practice Jesus' words every day! "Father, forgive them!" While that might not seem very fair to you, you have some promises that are included here. You will inherit the earth, you will be forgiven, and your kindness just may lead some of these mean girls to repent. Who knows?

## COMFORTABLE

Your task is probably the most revolutionary of all, because you hold within your current "healthiness" the ability to immediately bring healing to others! This is likely to make you some new friends—it will likely also make you some enemies. That's okay. Jesus told His disciples that the world hated Him . . . it'll hate us, too. Your first job is to run interference for the targets. If you see someone being targeted, you need to jump in there. Check out the story in the next chapter. Now go and be like Russ and Clay. Secondly, leave the comfort of your routine and begin seeking out the lonely. Sit with someone who always sits alone. Invite someone lonely to do something outside of school. It's what Jesus did. It's radical. And it's likely to be one of the most rewarding experiences of your life!

CHAPTER 7

# REVOLUTION

In 1994 I was teaching fifth grade in Tulsa, Oklahoma. It was my first teaching job, and I loved the kids in that class! It was actually a team situation where I taught English and math and Mr. Hoover taught science and history. Perfect. Fifty brilliant kids shuffling in and out of my room every day . . . and I loved each and every one of them. But you've been to school, so you know they didn't necessarily love one another.

Two of my favorite students that year were ornery, athletic boys named Clay and Russ. (Okay, yes, teachers have favorites . . .) Clay and Russ were popular kids, hardworking students, and just plain fun to have around. There was another student in my classroom that year whom I'll call Jeffry.

Jeffry had some verbal disabilities, finding it hard to begin sentences. He struggled with school, had unruly hair, was not athletic . . . You get the picture. He was a natural-born target.

Jeffry reminded me of a classic *Far Side* cartoon in which one deer is standing talking with another in the middle of a forest. One of the deer has a red bulls-eye right in the middle of his chest, and the other deer simply states, "Bummer of a birthmark, Hal."

One day during recess I walked into the hallway to find Jeffry running as hard as he could, tears streaming down his face, toward the boys' bathroom. Behind him were two girls looking a bit concerned. I allowed Jeffry to go past and stopped the girls. "What's up, ladies?"

The girls informed me that Clay and Russ had been teasing Jeffry on the playground and things had gotten a bit out of hand. I told the girls I'd take care of Jeffry—they were to send Clay and Russ to me. I wasn't sure what I would say yet, but I knew it couldn't be a typical "Go directly to jail—do not pass Go—do not collect $200" talk. That approach often doesn't change anything, and we needed to see a change. Clay and Russ appeared in the hallway looking like whipped puppies with their tails between their legs. They figured they were dead meat. And wouldn't you know it—along came God riding on that white horse to rescue me at just the right moment. "I hear you guys were picking on Jeffry out there."

Heads nodded, but no eyes left the floor.

"He's pretty easy to pick on, huh, guys?"

Again heads nodded—small smirks on their faces and this time I received eye contact.

"Guys, I'm really surprised at you. You're athletes. You're on a team. What happens if you're playing football and no one blocks for the runner? He's gonna get creamed, right? And what if someone puts a late hit on your quarterback? You're going to try to punish that guy with *your* next hit, right?" Clay and Russ were digging all this football talk—they knew it was true, too. In sports we call that watching your teammate's back.

"Jeffry's on your team," I reminded them. "If he goes down, we all go down. That's the way it works. So the next time I hear about a fight on the playground, this is how I want it to go down: I want to hear that someone ELSE was picking on Jeffry and that you two stepped in, placing yourselves physically between that bully and Jeffry. And I want to hear that you two said . . ." What I did next could have resulted in lawsuits and the loss of my job had Clay and Russ not perceived it as the coolest thing a teacher had ever done to them . . .

"I want to hear that you two said" . . . and here I pushed Clay and Russ with all my might—okay, not all my might; that may have killed them—but with a lot of my might into the lockers behind them. If you could have seen it in slow motion, their cheeks would have looked like a running bull-dog, drool oozing out from beneath their cheek flaps, eyes wide with surprise, bodies shaking in the aftermath . . . They thought it was the sweetest thing ever!

"I want to hear that you two said, 'Hey! That's Jeffry, and he's with us. If you want to get to him you'll need to come through us first.' " And then I sent the two boys, bewildered that they had seemingly escaped punishment, back to the playground.

After recess, with Jeffry all calmed down and back in class, the two boys approached me. They wanted to know if I could move Jeffry's desk into their group. As you can imagine, Jeffry was not too excited about this arrangement. He looked like he was about to face a firing squad. Much to his disappointment, I moved him to Clay and Russ's table. The remainder of the year, these three worked as a group. Clay and Russ helped Jeffry with class, they worked with him at recess—teaching him to better throw and catch a ball— they invited him to spend the night, to go to movies . . .

At the end of each year the fifth grade class ran a timed mile to complete their PE training. I foolishly agreed to run with the class. Speedy little Luke, he came in well under seven minutes. Clay and Russ were not far behind him.

I straggled in at around eight minutes—not many were behind me. But Jeffry was. By nine minutes we were all in and beginning to worry about him. Nine and a half minutes revealed Jeffry at the final turn of the track, coming into view around the edge of the school building. His hair was absolutely plastered to his head, his face red and strained with exhaustion, his shirt wet and transparent with sweat . . . It didn't look like he'd make it . . .

And that's when my revolutionaries snapped to attention. "Come on, guys," Clay and Russ addressed the class. "We're bringing him in!" Like an army, the entire class ran out to where Jeffry struggled and finished the race with him. Talk about a tearjerker!

School is out! Boy + ~~its~~ it's about time. School is going to be great next year. No more Gena, no more Jara; boy what a blast. I'm not sorry I called Gina a (bleep), 'cause she is one. I hate her and so do many other people. May she die!! And the same goes for Jessica!

*It was really boring all day long, and the best part was chapel. It was fun to sing with the choir again. Real fun. In a way I'm sorry that I didn't make the Student Life Committee. I love God more than anything, no matter how much I get in trouble. I LOVE GOD!!!*

"With the tongue we praise our Lord and Father, and with it we curse human beings, who have been made in God's likeness. Out of the same mouth come praise and cursing. My brothers and sisters, this should not be. Can both fresh water and salt water flow from the same spring? My brothers and sisters, can a fig tree bear olives, or a grapevine bear figs? Neither can a salt spring produce fresh water." James 3:9–12 TNIV

When I first found and reread my diary (as an adult) I was struck dumb by the correlation between what I had written and what James had written. Within the space of one three-and-a-half-by-four-inch page I had become the perfect poster child for James 3!

> With the tongue we praise our Lord and Father—
> *I LOVE GOD*!!! And with it we curse human beings,
> who have been made in God's likeness—*may she die*!!

I think I wanted everyone to see me as that fig tree, bearing big, beautiful ripe figs for all who were hungry to come and partake of . . . but I was the only one who was unable to see that I wasn't even *producing* figs!

James begins this verse by nailing us with our sin. You and I both know that the dual personality of the tongue is a universal in the world of girls. We've got our mouths shooting off in two directions all the time. We may even contradict ourselves within a matter of minutes.

```
Terri is the target today. Her shirt is
definitely too tight.
```

```
After she passes, you laugh with the others
and agree that she's a you-know-what.
```

```
After class, Terri asks you for a ride to
youth group tonight.
```

```
You smile and say, "Yeah! That'll be so fun!"
```

After school you promise the others you won't invite Terri to your party.

At youth group you sit with Terri. She is in your small group.

The altar call has you both in tears. You hug and pray for each other.

When you drop Terri off at home you promise to call her tomorrow.

The next day you mail your party invitations. You have not sent one to Terri.

So which is it? Are you a friend of Terri or are you a non-friend? It's plain to see, isn't it, that there is no way to say, "I'm both!" and then to defend your claim with any integrity. A friend doesn't slander. Which was real—the slander or the hugs and tears? Which was real—my love of God or my hatred toward Gina? In His kindness, God moves us to make a final choice.

Clay and Russ caused an absolute revolution in my classroom. They changed Jeffry's world. They influenced me, and now they have inspired you. I'm sure that when they decided to build rather than to destroy, those 11-year-old boys had no idea that their story would end up in a book—a book for girls at that! But that's what a revolution does. On whose world will your revolution have an impact?

## THE REVOLUTIONIST'S PLEDGE

I pledge to start a Revolution.

My tongue is a dangerous weapon,

But I will use it to murder no more.

My tongue is a fire—

I will use it only to ignite the

altar of praise.

My tongue **is** small,

and yet it can cause great damage—

I will use it instead to bind up those

who are wounded.

I pledge to be the defender of the accused.

I will stand in the gap for the girl

who is abused.

I will be silent no more.

This is not a pledge of popularity,

but of absolute revolt

And I pledge to start a Revolution.

CHAPTER 8

# REBELLION:
## LOOKING FOR INDEPENDENCE

➡ I SAID:

January 28: Crid, Bryan and I were home alone. We smoked and had beer and whisky. I don't know how we hid the smell.

February 5: Mom brought it up today that she thought Crid and Bryan were getting in trouble. She didn't directly mention me, but she knows. Not that I do it all the time; she just thinks I did it because Chris and Buz were there. Well the joke's on her, because I plan to do it more and I want to try pot also.

March 29: Today was never ending in the school department. We had a social studies test that I thought I did good on, but I got an 80%. I got a B+ on my science test, but I copied off of Peggy, so thats nothing. I'm afraid I'm turning into a B student.

→ YOU SAID:

Recently, someone that knows me really well and loves me said that I'm not consciously rebelling, but the music I listen to and the clothes I wear can be rebellion also, because my parents didn't tell me that I could, but didn't tell me that I couldn't, and I know that they'd love for me to change. Right now, I have been taking a good look at myself and seeing if this is really who I am, and really who I want people to see me as by the way I dress and the things I like. I grow closer to God daily. I spend a lot of time asking Him to show me who I really am and to draw me closer to Him and keep me on the straight and narrow.

ALEX, GEORGIA

MY period of rebellion was the worst few months of my life. I didn't exactly hate everyone around me and start doing drugs or drinking. NO, no, no, my rebellion was against God. I felt like He was letting me down in everything I would try. I went to school and started getting bad grades; I felt like I didn't know God as well as I used to. I think the worst part was that, not feeling God's fire inside me so I turned against Him and went with what the world was doing. I had used to be such an outgoing, loud, funny, exciting Christian and now I was a quiet, sad introvert. The worst part was that my friends had started to notice it. They thought I was going through a depression. Well, whatever it was, I knew it was unhealthy. Everything that came out of my mouth started to become negative, my image of myself, my image of my friends, and my image of my God. I didn't think that anyone could help me until one day my friends confronted me and told me that something was different about me and maybe I should try reading the Bible again. I resisted at first thinking that God hadn't helped me before and why would He help me now. But one day I just gave up and broke down and started praying to God for help, and He showed me that I had let go of Him, not that He had ever let go of me. I began reading my Bible again and He has opened up so many doors of love and hope ever since then.

KAITLYN, OHIO

Since I am the age that I am, I guess it isn't so much 24-7, but there are sometimes that I'm just like, no I don't want to, I'm going to do it my own way. When I am like that it gets really hard to have a good, strong relationship with God.

BLAIRE, 12

I have a big attitude problem, I'll admit it, and I would use things against my mom that really had nothing to do with her. I would take my anger and frustrations out on her. God drew me out of rebellion. Realizing my worth in His eyes and becoming more active in church have really brought me out of that stage.

JENNIFER, 17

I've gone against my parents' wishes a lot of times, with a lot of things, boys mostly though. Nothing really drew me out of it. It was more a spiritual awakening that brought me out of Satan's grasp. He had me in check for about 3 or 4 months of my 8th grade year. God saves, and I'm a proven image of His true forgiveness. I love the Lord with my whole heart, soul, and mind, and I love others as myself, and that's what we're called to do. People ask, "What's my sole purpose in life?" That's your answer, to love the Lord your God with everything in you, and to love others as yourself. You've fulfilled God's plan if you follow those two easy guidelines. So, God brought me out of my traps. And He won't let me fall again.

MORGAN, 14

*Rebellion has never really actually entered into the picture for me. Usually I think about rebelling with some things or people, but then never really had the courage to actually do it. If I had really rebelled, like talking back to teachers or parents, I would probably get myself into a sticky situation. Sometimes just getting that voice inside your head that tells you it wouldn't be the Christian thing to do saves me from doing it.*

*TEKA, 13, CALIFORNIA*

Rebellion is a funny thing. I mean, let's face it: At some point we have all been flat-out rotten! I guess you could say it's kind of fun at the time, that feeling of elation you get when it seems like you're taking a big risk, telling the entire world just where it can go and just what it can do . . . but then it all comes crashing down, doesn't it? I know it didn't take me too long to figure out that every move I made was soon found out by "the authorities" . . . my mom, my teachers . . . even my friends! They weren't as dumb as television makes them out to be, you know?

There were some striking similarities in the comments on rebellion that girls from all over the country sent to me:

You always <u>KNEW</u> you were in rebellion

Most of your rebellion was admittedly against God or your parental units

Your relationship with God was <u>NOT</u> good
during this time of rebellion

There was a certain emptiness your rebellion
brought about; you grew tired of it at
some point

In nearly every case, a good friend cared
enough to confront you, and this was the
beginning of the end of your bad behavior


One of the worst times of rebellion I encountered was long after I wrote my middle school diary. In fact, I was actually a Christian college student when I went through this desert of sorts—I look at the checklist above and I can see that I fit into each and every category.

It was the summer of 1986 and I was working for a "summer stock" theater company near Boston. As far as I was concerned, there were two strikes currently against me—one was that I was working as a box office manager, not as an actor. This was definitely a pride issue. I don't know about you, but I always seem to have this short list of really cool jobs in my head, and if I'm not doing one of the "really cool jobs"—like animal trainer at the zoo, drummer in a touring rock band, or being the boss of something—then I tend to downplay what I do. So yeah, I was just the box office person. The second strike was that I had just lost my first love.

I had invested a lot in my first love. Two years of my life were spent chasing this beautiful troubled actor. He said he planned on marrying me. I certainly planned on marrying him. We just had to get him over that pesky problem of his potentially liking guys more than he liked girls and we'd be good to go. I guess I thought I could change him.

When it ended I was devastated. I was embarrassed. I curiously found myself at the brink of paranoia—I thought for some reason that everyone knew all of the crazy things I had tried in order to keep this relationship together. I thought everyone stood back shaking their heads and whispering compassionately to one another, "I can't believe she just wasted two years of her life like that." And I didn't want their compassion or pity. I really didn't. I wanted to seem strong and in control. Pride again.

Pride hitting the wall makes for an ugly scene. Here's some twisted thinking for you. I decided that since I was apparently unlovable, I would take advantage of the fact that for the first time in my life I was in a town far, far away from home where no one knew me. A reasonable proposition would be something like this: I just touched the stove. The stove was hot and I got burned. I won't ever touch a hot stove again. But this proposition doesn't make so much sense: I just lost my first love. I feel hurt. I know! I'll throw out everything I've ever trusted and believed and live instead like a heathen!

I tried my hardest that summer to get in trouble—I really did. I hung out with all the wrong people. I laughed at and told all the wrong jokes. I drank the wrong beverages. I led three different guys to believe that they might be able to have summer flings with me . . .

All I can say is, praise God that those five similarities mentioned in the checklist above were operating in overdrive for me that summer.

I knew I was wrong—in fact, I'm pretty sure it's downright <u>illegal</u> to change the birth date on your driver's license . . .

I was mad at God for my broken relationship. Isn't that crazy? He rescued me from a marriage that would have been a certain disaster and I was angry . . .

I did not crack open my Bible all that summer, nor did I cry out to Him in prayer. (Not on my own volition, anyhow.)

I was miserable! I felt dirty, guilty, lonely . . . and embarrassed still.

God threw me the life ring just in time . . .

It's so odd how God chooses to rescue us in our rebellion. By the end of the summer I was beside myself with misery. It's hard to believe that in the course of only ten weeks' time one can hate who she has become, but some of you know what I'm talking about. On top of everything else, though I did not know it yet, I had contracted mononucleosis and would have to miss the first few weeks of my junior year of college—and, as a result, the opportunity to perform in an amazing production of *Godspell*.

Our bawdy troupe of summer performers had been bunking, ironically, in an old Catholic monastery. One night we were informed that another group would be sharing the facility, so we should mind our p's and q's (that's old-time talk for "mind your manners") . . . Turns out the other group was a troupe of Christian actors who traveled about and did "skits." I can remember participating in a "mocking" session at lunch. Were they serious? Christian skits? How stupid was that?

Later that night I heard sounds in the monastery's great room—a large activity area that was rarely used by our own theater company. It was the touring group. I stood back in the shadows watching the touring company for a while, knowing full well that I had spent the summer pretending to be someone with whom I was very uncomfortable. I was a poser and I hated how unsettled I felt. I don't know what compelled me, but I stepped out of the shadows and approached a small group of actors who were sitting on a group of couches at the edge of the room.

I am not a crier—check that one out with my family. I married a man who will sit for hours watching *Anne of Green Gables* or *The Waltons* and simply cry himself a river. I am the stoic of the family. Yet here I was, hundreds of miles from home, surrounded by a group of absolute strangers and crying like a baby. I confessed it all—the guys, the drinking, my embarrassment and pride, the conflict I was having with my faith, my broken heart—I was simply listened to and loved upon. It was, I must say, a lifegiving moment.

GOD'S DIARY

My mom, a psychologist by trade, has always said that some measure of teenage rebellion is to be expected and is even necessary. She would often tell me when I was a teenager that she worried about my friends who had never experienced any form of rebellion. This is a common psychological teaching —teenagers are going through a period of asserting their independence from their parents and need to offer some form of revolt in order to do this. As a Christian psychologist, my mom said that without this separation a teen would never make her own choice about a relationship with Christ.

There's definitely some evidence for this in Scripture. The prodigal son (Luke 15) had to leave home to discover he really did want to be his father's son. King David was called a man after God's own heart; he once had a cheatin' heart though (2 Samuel 11), and never wanted to do that again. And Peter was one of the lead figures in the birth of the church, but only after he put on his tough-guy, I-never-knew-Him (Matthew 26) act and had to be put back together by Jesus, Humpty Dumpty style (John 21:15–17)

So rebellion can have some good aftereffects. Perhaps there is truth in the idea that unless we mount some sort of mutiny we will never have a desire to walk on the straight and narrow. Even Jesus said, "He who has been forgiven little loves little." James Dobson said that rebellion in teens is "like a tornado that drops unexpectedly out of a dark sky, tyrannizes a family, shakes up the community and then blows on by. Then the sun comes out and spreads its warmth again."[1]

But I don't want to appear pro-rebellion, so let me throw this thought out there. Many people will say that rebellion is normal. It is a normal thing for teens to be angry and not really understand why. It is normal to question your parents. It is normal to want to make your own decisions, especially about clothes, music, and friends. It's normal to feel irritated a lot. And do you remember what else I've pointed out as normal? Sin. The sin nature is what is normal in our flesh, so we can't simply embrace what is normal and tell everyone who is unfortunate enough to get in our way, "Deal with it!"

"Normal" and "good" can sometimes work together, but it's important for us to realize that they don't always work together, and they are certainly not the same thing. For instance, my dog loves to eat a lot of "normal" dog things. He likes rawhide bones, dog biscuits, all kinds of meat, and cat poop. If this were Sesame Street I could start singing "One of These Things Is Not Like the Other" right now, and you would very quickly discern that the answer to this song's riddle is CAT POOP!! That's just gross. When Biscuit (my dog) eats the first three things mentioned, I watch him proudly and say stupid things like, "Aww, isn't he cute?" But when he is eating cat poop I gag, lunge at him, and scold him . . . as if I could ever convince him that this is not a delicacy. All four of those things are normal for a dog to eat. Wouldn't you agree with me that all four are not good?

Thirteen-year-old Taylor Anne from Georgia decided she would try to find a way to merge rebellion and obedience. Here's what she came up with:

*I personally am sort of in an eternal state of rebellion. Certainly not against God or my parents, but against today's society. Sex on the radio, drugs in the rock n roll, violence in the streets, rights being taken away, girls tearing each other up inside just to get higher and more well known. Please, if you want to be well known, do something BESIDES what everyone else in the world is falling under to. Being in this alternative lifestyle seriously brought me closer to God. I mean, isn't that what being a Christian is partially about? Being different from the rest of the universe? Church punks can DEFINITELY change the world, and believe you me, we're doing it!*

So we have established that rebellion, while normal, is not necessarily good. It may be helpful (in the long run) as it helps us to establish our own identity in Christ, but just as "normal" and "good" are not the same thing . . . neither are "helpful" and "good." Today is the perfect day to begin bringing the rebellion in your life to its knees. It won't happen overnight and you may experience some setbacks. But if you desire to take control of rebellion in your life . . . then it has already achieved its purpose. Like so much of life, it can bring us healing only after it has first sickened us.

## MY STRUGGLE

This might require some guts from you, but I want you to have a talk with three people.

1. Talk with God. Ask Him to show you where your greatest struggle with rebellion lies. It may not even be something you have recognized before today. But ask Him to show you where you have been fighting Him and others the most lately.

2. Talk with a good friend who not only knows you well, but who is NOT (as far as you can tell) struggling with rebellion in her life. Ask her the same question. Where does she see you struggling the most? Has she ever prayed that an attitude or behavior of yours would change? Be sure you pray together after you talk. Is there anything sweeter than two friends actually building each other up?

3. Talk with your mom or dad . . . your primary parent or guardian. What is the biggest area of rebellion they see in your life? Now, be prepared, because your asking this question is likely to blow them away! But be humble as well. They may really surprise you with their answer. You may expect them to mention a certain friend of yours only to find them addressing your attitude about helping around the house. Are you ready, whatever it is, to lay it down?

You may possibly need to have a fourth talk. Read 1 Corinthians 15:33. What are the first four words?

This is one of those verses that really challenge us, because as human beings we were created to be in fellowship/relationship with one another. And part of the sweetness of being a teenager is having so many friends and beginning to know the freedom of "hanging out." But it may be that as you deal with rebellion, it will require the laying down or the surrender of an actual friendship. That is a tremendous sacrifice, and not one that I take lightly, but then again, God does say (in some versions), "Do not be deceived . . ."

"Well my one friend who I was closest to in that group had moved, and honestly I'm kinda glad she did. I don't know if I would've stuck with that group or not. She's a great person and a really good friend. She was just into some stuff that I wish she wasn't in. I talked to her about it and she lightened up but I don't think she ever stopped."

CHAPTER 9

## MOM WAS RIGHT:

## LOOKING FOR HEALING

➤ I SAID:

February 6: We had basketball until 5:30 and when I got home I did homework and watched t.v. Mom is starting to get on my case about watching too much T.V. I think she's crazy. I like T.V. and I won't give it up!

February 8: Mom is being a real (bleep!) lately. She says I won't tell her what I think; well, I'm one of those people who put their feelings down on paper instead of pouring them out to some "friend."

February 14: Well, Mom just saw Vegas and picked it apart so bad I can't watch it anymore. I think she's crazy. I'll find a way to still see it.

February 22: When I write in my diary, I'm usually in bed. It's kind of funny 'cause each night when I get into bed I have to straighten the covers. Mom gets mad 'cause I never make my bed. Well, that's the way the bed bounces. HA! HA!

March 9: I don't know whose leg I'm trying to pull with my stealing stunt. Mom knows I did it, though she never comes right out and says anything. She did confront me with it today, but I denied it. God knows and I'm sorry, so that's all that matters.

April 5: Boy, Mom's really boring at night. "The Barefoot Man and His Band" play nightly here and they're really good. But oh no, Mom won't go in there because it's a nightclub. But she's not so bad in the daytime.

I'VE NEVER BEEN SO ~~████~~
IN MY LIFE! Just so my brother
could make 15 ~~████~~ dollars, I
have to get up 3 HOURS EARLY
AND GO TO CHURCH. I'M ~~████~~
It's been ONE ~~████~~ ROTTEN
DAY. We took Loni and Russ out
to eat AND LONI AND RICK WERE
BOTH ~~████~~ I'm so ~~████~~. I
just have to cool down, but I
can't. I mean I get to sleep in
2 DAYS a week. Now it's only
one. I'M mad. VERY, VERY,
VERY ~~████~~!

→ YOU SAID:

My relationship with my mom isn't a very
close relationship. We have drifted so far
away from each other than when I was a
little girl. I miss those times but now it seems
we fight so much more. Lately though, we have

been getting along better and setting some things straight . . . kind of like a fresh start. I'm glad I am slowly getting closer to her because I know when she's gone, she's gone and I will regret why I wasn't closer to her.

TYLER-MICHELLE, 15

It seems as though my mother and I have a very odd relationship. We love each other, but sometimes we hate to get along. On occasion, we find ourselves saying things to each other so we can hurt the other member of the party. And while I know she loves me, I feel as though sometimes our relationship is strained and I can't tell her how I feel. If there is one thing I truly regret about how my life is pre-college, it's the fact I never grew closer to my mother.

MOLLY

I wish I would've gotten to know my mom sooner, but it wasn't until this past year that we really began to bond. Now we talk about everything, laugh together, pray together, read the same books, and watch the same movies. We're best friends. It's really helped me to keep myself in check too. Now it's

easier for me to figure out what I should
and shouldn't be doing or watching because
I know that if I wouldn't want her there for
it, I probably shouldn't be doing it. I'm so
thankful to have a mom and friend like her,
I wouldn't have it any other way.

WHITNEY S.


My relationship with my mom is mostly great.
Of course there are times when we get on
each other's nerves and I get disrespectful.
I feel like I can tell her a lot but some
things I feel that she would just not understand, even though she probably does. I
see her as a godly woman and a stronger
woman. I hope that one day I have the
motherly wisdom that she has. But the best
part of our relationship is that we can laugh
together about the most stupidest things.
It's great!

JULIE R., 18


The relationship with my mom isn't the best.
We argue a lot and occasionally we'll have
a good day and be fine with each other but
that doesn't happen very often. Actually on
Thursday night we got in an argument because

I didn't call her and tell her I was going to get my oil changed after school. I was even with my dad which I don't understand why she got so mad, but Thursday nights I go to my dad's house and I told her I was going over there and she said no. She told me to go to my room and of course being the rebel that I am I said no, I'm leaving. Well then she said if you leave you aren't coming back . . . Well I left and now I live with my dad. I haven't talked to her since. The thing that bugs me the most about her is that she always tries to get on my last nerves. Like when I'm not in a good mood and she'll get all in my face and try to be funny but it's just really annoying!

BROOKE

I know that for girls my age, a good relationship with their moms is not common. My mom and I have always had a wonderful relationship and we have always been able to talk and share things that are going on in our lives. My mom is the one person that I can go to whenever I have a problem or need advice. I can always count on her to be there for me when it seems like no one else cares. My mom is right about a lot, and even though I hate to admit it she knows better than I do. So I would like to say, Mom, I love you and thank you for always being there for me.

KAITLYN, 14

## IMPRINTING

(Suzy) I just came from what is, these days, an all-too-typical visit with my mom. I pulled into town at midnight; Fort Wayne, Indiana, happened to be right in between two speaking engagements. By one thirty I fell into bed, resolving to get up early so we could spend some time hanging out the next day. Early turned into nine in the morning (I know, that still sounds pretty early for many of you, but I had hoped by some miracle maybe I could be up by eight). After a couple of hours of chatting with Mom and Dad, my family began to arrive, and by lunchtime there were seventeen of us looking for a table at a Chinese restaurant. Three o'clock was the designated hour of departure, so there I was, only fifteen hours after my arrival, backing

SLOWLY OUT OF THE DRIVEWAY AND FLASHING THE
AMERICAN SIGN LANGUAGE "I LOVE YOU" TO MOM
AND DAD, PROMISING THAT NEXT TIME I VISIT IT
WILL BE FOR LONGER . . .

In 1979 my mom and I had a lot of hang-out time available to us. In fact, the typical Saturday night, any Saturday night really, found me curled up on the couch with some sort of junk food, in the dark, surrounded by big fluffy pillows and waiting for the start of what I thought was the greatest TV show ever . . . *The Love Boat*! What an amazing show! First, Gopher was on the show every week—that was a given—and he was a FOX! Secondly, I could count on at least one other foxy guest star per week. There is one page in my diary where I had even cut a small picture of an actor named Michael Lembeck from the *TV Guide* (most recently the director of *The Santa Clause 3*) and pasted him at the bottom of the page. Above his picture I wrote *FOX*! This weekly appearance of various foxy guest stars enabled me to ignore the fact that a lot of the other guest stars on *The Love Boat* were well over fifty years old (which I then thought to be ancient) and therefore completely lame guest stars.

So where does hang-out time with Mom come into the picture? Well, I suppose something in the very title *Love Boat* set off her internal mom-alarm and she felt that if I was going to watch a show where each week perfect strangers would meet one another within the first fifteen-minute segment of the show and wake up together in the same ship's cabin during the second fifteen-minute segment (fight during the third segment and make up during the fourth—that was the formula), perhaps she should be near me and give a running color commentary on what she saw. She drove me nuts! I could never just enjoy the show. It had to be punctuated every commercial break with comments like, "You know, it's not drug use that is going to destroy this country, it's all of this casual treatment of sex." Or, "This show is so clever at making something as perverted as casual sex look so sophisticated and normal." And the thing that bothered me most about Mom's commentary was . . . I knew she was right!

My mom was almost always right, and it *always* drove me up a wall. I didn't want her to be right when being right flew in the face of what I wanted to do and the way I wanted to live my life. I didn't want my decisions to be evaluated or scrutinized . . . but do you know what the funny thing is? Now that I look back I realize my mom didn't really evaluate or scrutinize *me* at all! It was simply a matter of this . . . no matter which direction I ran there was still a bond that I had with my mom. We were still attached, in a manner of speaking, and what was actually happening was I had gotten used to filtering my choices and decisions through what I thought Mom might say! After all, we had spent all of those preteen years talking in the car, and in my room before lights out, and as we drove home from church or a restaurant. I knew exactly what my mom believed about nearly every situation a girl could possibly find herself in. As a result, I could make a bad decision, be really upset with myself for it, and though she made no comment on it whatsoever, I would become mad at *her*. How bizarre!

There is actually a psychological thing happening here; it's called imprinting. After years of Mom's influence and instruction, I had adopted a lot of the same views and beliefs she held. I did a lot of things in the same manner as she. All mammals imprint, beginning at birth, which explains why my cat, which was abandoned by her mother at five weeks, chases soccer balls in the backyard. She was socialized not by a kitty mother, but by a three-month-old puppy that was much larger than she. She does not understand her size or the prescribed roles of a cat in this world. She believes herself, more or less, to be a dog. One of my favorite stories about imprinting comes from former *Saturday Night Live* actress Gilda Radner about her cousin's dog:

It wasn't an expensive dog, and it was pregnant. It apparently wasn't a very fast dog, either, because it ended up getting in the way of a lawn mower.

The dog lost its two hind legs but was saved when the owners rushed her to a veterinarian who gave the owners two choices: He could stitch up the dog and let it live with only two legs, or he could put the dog down. If the dog was stitched up, the puppies she carried would be born, no problem. If the dog died, then, obviously, the puppies would die too.

Radner's cousin told the vet to stitch up the dog, and here's what happened: "So the vet sewed up her backside," wrote Radner, "and over the next week the dog learned to walk. She didn't spend any time worrying, she just learned to walk by taking two steps in the front and flipping

> up her backside, and then taking two steps
> and flipping up her backside again."
>
> The surgically transformed dog gave
> birth to six perfectly healthy puppies. But
> here's the amazing thing: After she nursed
> and weaned the puppies, they learned to
> walk—and they all walked exactly like their
> mother! They each took two steps with their
> front paws and then flipped their backsides
> forward.[1]

Our world is so backwards today—we recognize Ms. Radner's story as an amazing example of imitation, and yet I know a lot of people would tell me that my mom had brainwashed me. That as a teenager I needed to "find my own truth" instead of "flipping my backside around" like my mom. There is partial truth in that statement. I did need, as we discussed in the last chapter, to make my *faith* my own. *Truth*, however, cannot be my own. Truth belongs to God, and it is universal. There is right and there is wrong. There is true and there is false. And the beauty about truth is that it does not require that *anyone* believe it in order to be Truth! My mom had taught me Truth using the Bible . . . and an insane amount of conversation. God had sealed that truth in my heart. I was free—because my God is a loving God and a gentleman—and because my mom chose not to live my life for me, I was free to walk away from Truth as much as I wanted to. But every time I did, His Spirit and all that Mom had taught me were already living there inside me, and my own little alarm would go off. I didn't need Mom's alarm any longer—that groundwork had been laid long ago.

The longer I live and the more I watch my mom in action I am aware of the great Mom-Truth: No one on earth really loves me like my mom. She has told me that for years, but of course I thought it was just her pride talking. Turns out it is true. It's not a statement of quantity . . . It's not like Mom loves me THIIIIIIIIIIIIIIIS much and my husband loves me THIIIIIIS much. They are different loves. Jonathan's always been friend, lover, and constant companion. He's my husband not only because he loves me, but also because he likes me. We chose each other, and we choose each other every single day.

Mom's never had the luxury of choosing me! I grew inside of her, knit together in the secret by God's design, and she had to be surprised by me like the rest of the world. She was able to shape and form me a great deal, but she could only work with the material that she was given. I am an introvert, an athlete, an animal lover, competitive, sometimes shy, sometimes sarcastic . . . Jonathan chose that. Mom was stuck with it . . . and yes, maybe helped develop it all a bit. And yet Mom loves me. She loves me with the fiercest of jealousies. God help the person that tries to mess with Mama's little girl, because my sweet little hundred-pound, 5'2" mother will become a force to reckon with. She is my biggest fan, my defender, and truest girl confidante. I pray that my beautiful daughters know that I strive to be nothing less for them . . . minus the hundred-pound part. I think that goal is long out of reach.

(Suzy) I WAS FLYING FROM TULSA, OKLAHOMA, TO FORT MYERS, FLORIDA, TO SPEND A WEEK AT THE BEACH WITH MY MOM. MY FLIGHT LEFT MIDMORNING, TAKING ME TO ATLANTA, GEORGIA,

WHICH WAS WHERE MOM'S LAYOVER WAS, TOO. WE
HAD TICKETS ON THE SAME FLIGHT FROM ATLANTA
TO FORT MYERS. I WAS CERTAIN MY FLIGHT LEFT
AT 11:00 A.M. AND HAD ARRANGED FOR FRIENDS TO
PICK ME UP AT 9:30. AT ABOUT 9:15 I WAS
PUTTERING AROUND THE KITCHEN AND HEARD A PLANE
FLYING LOW OVERHEAD . . . SUDDENLY I WAS MOVED
TO CHECK MY TICKETS. OBVIOUSLY YOU KNOW BY
NOW THAT I SHOULD HAVE CHECKED THE TICKETS
THE NIGHT BEFORE, FOR SURE ENOUGH THAT WAS
MY FLIGHT I HEARD BUZZING MY HOUSE! MY POOR
MOM ARRIVED ON TIME IN ATLANTA AND HAD TO
WAIT SIX HOURS FOR ME TO ARRIVE ON THE NEXT
FLIGHT. I FELT AWFUL! IN MY MIND I PLAYED OUT
ALL THE SCENARIOS OF HER DISAPPOINTMENT, HER
ANGER, HER PUNISHMENT. BUT WHEN I ARRIVED IN
ATLANTA AND WAS GREETED BY ONE TIRED MOMMY
. . . SHE MENTIONED THAT THE DAY HAD BEEN
LONG, BUT THAT WAS ABOUT IT. SHE HUGGED ME
AND LET ME KNOW THAT SHE WAS REALLY LOOKING
FORWARD TO OUR VACATION TOGETHER. I DESERVED
HER WRATH—BUT SHE GAVE ME MERCY.

I'm proud to say, I have a pretty good
relationship with my mom. She is the best
mom ever. We're not super rich or anything,
but whenever I want something like a new

shirt or some cash, she's happy to oblige.
I went to Fine Arts in Orlando, Florida,
and I brought my mom's new digital camera.
My friends and I went to Disney World and
we were in line for a rollercoaster when I
realized that my bag was wet. When I opened
it up, I saw that my small carton of milk had
been punctured by one of my pens. The milk
was everywhere and, to my great horror,
had drenched my mother's camera. I knew
I had to tell her before I got back home. I
called her that night, and she said accidents
happened! She just waved it off and said that
I was more important than any camera, no
matter how much it had cost! I was so happy.
My mom is the best!

CHANI, TEXAS

## WHEN MOM'S NOT THERE TO TEACH

The thing is . . . we have a problem with this whole mother/daughter relationship thing today, don't we? Mothers and daughters are not merely suffering from a minor ability to relate to one another. In many cases mothers are only fifteen years or so older than their daughters—both from the same generation. They do indeed like the same music, wear the same clothes, and sometimes—if Jerry Springer is accurate—they are attracted to the same guys. Mothers are increasingly having to raise families on their own, working longer hours and remaining absent from the home. There is an increase of woman-on-woman violence—I'm meeting more and more girls whose mothers are in jail due to abuse charges as well as drug and alcohol use. Divorced women date, inviting boyfriends to spend the night in a home where young girls live. I have met girls all around the country who deal with each of these issues.

It's happening to the guys, too. Donald Miller—an author you really need to read—has written an entire book called To Own a Dragon: Reflections on Growing Up without a Father. When interviewed by Crosswalk.com, a Web site designed to hook you up with all kinds of Bible studies, devotions, CD and movie reviews, and interviews, Miller talked about how missing a parent—either parent—can really slow down our growth. Crosswalk asked Miller if there are life-lessons or self-beliefs that a boy just won't get without a father.

> MILLER: The biggest one is that he is affirmed and loved. Not going to learn that without a dad. Probably not going to learn it well without a mom, for that matter. It's just a necessary component of upbringing to our well-being, to have a father say, "You're loved, I love you, I care about you." I long for that every day.

I wish I had a dad who would say that. I'm 34, and I still want that. It's not going to go away. There are other people who do that in our lives and that's great, and everybody walks around with some sort of pain, some sort of wound, so I'm not playing the victim card here, but that's the big one.

So yeah, there are things you will not learn unless you have a father in your home. That said, it's not a hopeless case. I didn't have a father in my home, and I write books, have a great life, teach at a school, interact with people, have good friends. But that's because there were mentors in my life that taught me certain things. What I wanted to do with this book was go through what I had to learn else-where having grown up without a father. I missed out on so much, from how to deal with money, to how to make decisions, to how to talk to and engage a woman.[2]

There's no doubt that God designed girls to be cared for by our mothers, and that care is intended to last well into our adulthood, at least by virtue of receiving her compassion, her encouragement, and her wisdom. But I'm sure you don't need me to tell you that this really isn't a perfect world. There are a lot of people out there who never did have this experience, and you may be one of them. My own daughters are.

I never grew up with a mom wanting to do makeup with me. Going through junior high and my first year of high school I never had a mom to talk about boys and drama at school with. It was so hard to grow up and hear people talk about how great their mom is and how she was their hero, because to be honest, my mom was not my hero. Sometimes I look back on my childhood and wish I could say that I have all of those amazing experiences that most little girls have. I might not have had the mom that most girls have, but God put other women in my life that tried to be a mom to me. I rejected most of them. I felt that if my biological mom did not want me, why would some random woman with no relation to me want me? It made no sense to me. They loved me so much more than my mom did, yet I could not see why, so I decided they were fake and unreal. These were my feelings on women as mother figures until I met Suzy. I was in a bathroom crying; she hugged me and listened to me. At that moment I felt something different. Over the past year Suzy and I have grown very close. Moving to Pennsylvania was the biggest jump of my life. Suzy, even though she has no relation to me by blood, she is my mom. She is more motherly and more understanding than my mom ever was. She hugs me and comforts me. She teases me and laughs with me. She is my mom and I love her.

RACHAEL, 15

For the information of anyone reading this, my name is Marie Weibel. Since the ripe age of three months I have been "motherless." That's not to say I haven't had a woman figure in my life from time to time, but it is to say I have never had that woman. The one that gave me life, and the one that "lucky" people call Mom.

My mother was twenty-four with three other kids all in different places when I was born. From the moment I drew my first breath I was an inconvenience to her life. She was an alcoholic, a drug addict with little money, and no husband. Though I have heard from her that she loved me from the time she laid eyes on me, she just couldn't handle taking care of me. So she in the end left me with my half-sister Rachael's father, where she thought I might have a better life. Sadly it wasn't a better life. This man that I called Dad was the same as my mom and then some.

He passed away when I was nine and left me not only motherless but fatherless as well. Yet the wound of having no mother hurt more than his departure. I have lost countless hours of sleep wondering what might be different if my mother would have kept me. I have wondered would she love me, would she be pleased at my choices in life, would she think I was beautiful, would she have taught me how to cook, and then another dozens of hours wondering what is her middle name, does she know my birthday, did I inherit any of her traits, does she laugh like me, who was her first crush, can she cook, is she sarcastic, where did she grow up, and what was it like? Did she go through all the drama I have—and lastly, does she ever wonder what her girl is like?

It has taken me awhile to get to this point in life where I realize I wouldn't be me if she were in my life. I wouldn't have had the life I have, and it wouldn't have been a better one. Sure the questions would be answered and the pain from her leaving wouldn't be there. But her keeping me wouldn't have changed her. I have also realized that I am more blessed than any one person who has their mother. True, they have a bond inseparable by anything, but I have seen the kindness of people, and the true love our Father has for us.

Since the time my dad died there has been someone who has cared for me and who has shown me that I am loved. If I really think about it, I have had at least six moms and four dads. The point is, God does not leave the motherless motherless, or the fatherless fatherless. He puts other people in our lives to take those places. Some of those people you may never come to think of as a parent, but instead as a good mentor. Others though will leave a mark on you and they will love you more than you can imagine and those are the ones who are the parents. If you just open your eyes you will see that if you are missing a parent, there is someone out there that is missing a daughter like you. Trust in God and He will lead you to them.

MARIE, 14

The question we are left with then is, is this hopeless? Is there a plan God has for me, or did everyone else get the goods and for some reason I'm the one with coal in my stocking? It's a legitimate question, and one that you actually need to find the answer to. Because until you decide that God means business when He says in Psalm 68:5, "A father to the fatherless, a defender of widows, is God in his holy dwelling," . . . until you decide that God means business you will forever be pouting about the cards you've been dealt, and maybe you'll fail to go on to see verse 6: "God sets the lonely in families."

I have so many friends who have been failed by parents. But I guess the reason they've made it to the point where they are OLD enough to be my friends . . . is that they have adopted older women as spiritual mothers and mentors and have chosen to identify with these women rather than with the one who initially imprinted on them. God alone has that power, because imprinting is a pretty powerful thing! Psychologist Konrad Lorenz, who first used the term "imprinting," once said that it was somehow "stamped irreversibly on the nervous system." Psychologists today, however, are beginning to say that imprinting is not so permanent after all—it's science catching up once again to God's word.[3] Because for thousands of years God has said, "If anyone is in Christ, behold! He is a new creation." That's my own creative punctuation, but check it out . . . you have the choice to be bitter, or to walk in freedom and actually become the amazing woman God created you to be!

There's no sense in carrying around anger over the family into which you were born, the circumstances that were presented you, or even the presence or absence of your mother. The past cannot be changed. But we can choose to say, "Okay, I'm going to trust God on this 'I'm sufficient. I'm enough' thing." If He's a father to the fatherless, then the motherless can make it, too.

# MY STRUGGLE

It's kind of interesting, the cycle that we go through with our moms. At birth, of course, we are totally dependant on her for everything—especially a loving touch and food, though that's gross to think about now. As we grow up she is kind of our hero. We dress up in her clothes, totter around in her shoes that are about a kajillion sizes too big for us, imitate the things that she says . . . Mom can basically do no wrong. When we hit about twelve, she can't do much right. She is embarrassing, overbearing, old-fashioned, too conservative . . . The list goes on and on. We begin to keep secrets from her, or at least dial down the truth a bit. Then when we come out on the other end we may share the sentiments of Mark Twain, who wrote in 1874 about his father: "When I was a boy of fourteen, my father was so ignorant I could hardly stand to have the old man around. But when I got to be twenty-one, I was astonished at how much he had learned in seven years."[4]

For a while in our adulthood we get to be true friends, financially independent of one another, both in the primes of our lives. Then toward the end of our time together, we are supposed to take her into our home, nurture her, hold her, comfort her, all those things she once did for us . . . It truly does come full circle.

What is the most amazing thing your mom has ever done for you?

Go tell her. Yeah. Right now. Call her on a cell phone if you're not at home! Relive that moment together. You'll bless her, because she's crazy about you. (And if it's not your mom, but a mentor . . . call her! She needs to know!)

CHAPTER 10

# GLAD I'M A GIRL?

## LOOKING FOR A FUTURE

→ I SAID:

February 2: I wish I was a boy instead of a girl. They have more rights, and they can run around with the "in" group even if they're ugly. And if they're good looking, they always have a girl.

March 18: I went over to the Marks's and took on Dan, Dave, and a friend of Dave's in Around the World. I was ahead of everyone until the end. They kept making comments about, "They're pretty bad if a girl can beat them." I felt really good hearing that, but at the same time I was thinking, "Who the (bleep) do they think they are?"

April 18: I just had a great experience! All of the girls who were here last night were really sharing themselves and there was a lot of crying. The exciting thing about it is that it was all centered on God. When we thought of how we were suffering, we realized that Christ must have gone through a lot more. All of us gave each other big hugs and we realized how close we all are.

June 12: We got the pants knocked off us by the Chicks. I let in 13 runs in three innings. Maybe the big leagues will sign me up, huh? Ha! I would love to. You know, I believe if I try hard and practice hard, I could make it. No one would approve, though, 'cause I'm a girl.

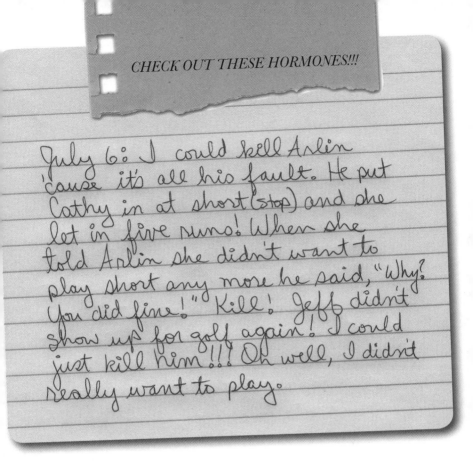

July 6: I could kill Arlin 'cause it's all his fault. He put Cathy in at short (stop) and she let in five runs! When she told Arlin she didn't want to play short any more he said, "Why? You did fine!" Kill! Jeff didn't show up for golf again! I could just kill him!!! Oh well, I didn't really want to play.

## → YOU SAID:

Guys have no problem fitting in and can talk to anyone; they also have no social rules and it doesn't matter who they hang out with all that much and they aren't judged as much as girls are. Girls are constantly trying to fit in and they are always being judged on how they look.

BECCA, 14

They can pee standing up and they can, for the most part, blow off drama without even giving it a second thought. When it comes to girls, the problems just kind of seem to hover for as long as possible, growing and getting as big as they can. Guys, for some reason unknown to me, have this ability to just kind of shrug off those things that girls always blow up and magnify.

WHITNEY

They get to do the "asking out" when they find interest in a girl. So basically they can have anyone. Also, guys seem to have it so much easier than us girls. They don't go through near as much as girls have to. Nor do they have to put up with all the drama and gossip. They just walk away. Or if it's a fight, one hit and it's over. Girls on the other hand drag out the cat fights like no other!

NICOLE B., 17

I've never considered myself jealous of boys. I've always been proud to be a girl. But I must say, I don't think it's fair that whenever a girl is mad or having a bad day, they blame it on PMS and not their own incompetence.

CHANI C., 16

I'm jealous of boys because they are boys. They think girls have it so easy. We don't. Plain and simple. Girls are complicated and I have yet to figure out why. Boys, from what I can tell, are out in the open and up front. I try to be that way but, to be honest, it's hard. It's probably easier for me since I'm around guys a lot and pick up a lot of their habits, but it's still hard to be open and up front whether I'm with guys or not.

BRE S., 15

It's not fair. Today after lunch all the boys went outside to play two-hand touch football and the other girls at my table said I wasn't allowed—I'm a girl. I didn't care, I went anyway because I didn't care, but that afternoon the girls wouldn't talk to me. I didn't care though; I had fun and made a new friend—Ryan!

JESSICA T., 14

Even now as I write this I am psyching myself up to tell you something embarrassing . . . Why should this be different from any other laughable diary moment? Somehow it *is* worse, but here goes: I really wanted to be a boy when I was growing up. I remember going into Mom and Dad's walk-in closet and . . .

coming out in my dad's three-piece suits. My best friend from across the street and I would sometimes pretend at night to be boxers (I have no idea why—I've never had even a slight interest in that sport . . .) and would make a boxing ring in one of our bedrooms; then we would spar with one another and pretend to knock each other out. Ugh, here's the embarrassing part . . . we would do this shirtless. (Take it easy—we were *ten* years old!) Oh, and you know how Michael J. Fox's character Marty McFly, in the *Back to the Future* trilogy, can't stand to be called "chicken"? Call McFly a chicken and he will stop dead in his tracks, clench his fists, squint his eyes, and slowly, determinedly turn to face his accuser. If anyone wanted me to have the same response, he (it was usually a he) only had to say something like, "You're pretty good for a girl." Ooh, my fists are clenching even now . . . it's hard to type with clenched fists!

So why would I be willing to share with you such embarrassing memories from my past? First of all, praise God, there does come a day and an hour in every mature woman's life where she realizes she is defined by who she is today, and not by any stupid thing done in the past . . . and believe me, we all have stupid moments. I trust it will only bring you and me closer! Secondly, I realize that there were some misunderstandings about God, the world, and women that I was entertaining, and that's what I want to talk about.

The male/female scales have never had a "fair" balance. We live in a society now that insists men and women receive equal time, equal pay, equal opportunity . . . and yet the historical truth runs something like this: Women have played a proportionally tiny part in the history of the arts and sciences. Even in the twentieth century, women got only

2 percent of the Nobel Prizes in the sciences—a proportion constant for both halves of the century—and 10 percent of the prizes in literature. The Fields Medal, the most prestigious award in mathematics, has been given to forty-four people since it originated in 1936. All have been men.[1]

I am not a feminist and do not want this to become the "feminism chapter," but the truth is there are certain things we just don't think of any longer, one hundred and fifty-five years after the birth of women's rights. At the time of the first Women's Rights Convention in 1848, women were not allowed to vote, they had no property rights, could be imprisoned or beaten by husbands with no legal protection, most professions and educational opportunities were closed to women . . . Even in 1979 when my granddaddy died, my grandma had a horrible time financially. When a person dies, any debts they may have are not automatically forgiven. Debts must be paid out of a person's estate. When Granddaddy died, his bank account was frozen so that anyone to whom he owed money could be sure to get their pay. The problem was that my grandma was on that bank account as well. She could not get to her own money! Grandma never dreamed of having her own savings account; she was Granddaddy's wife—the second name on the account. It wasn't a suppression of my grandma or her "rights" . . . it was just the way things were.

Part of my belief that boys had it better than girls was no doubt due to hearing my mom and others talk about stories such as Grandma's. But part of it was also based on my own observances:

Only boys were allowed to try out for Little League baseball; I tried out in disguise and made a team. They decided to keep me even after they found out I was female.

Boys were allowed to display their intelligence at school by getting good test grades and raising their hand for every question the teacher posed. Girls were considered intimidating if they did so.

Boys didn't have to deal with that pesky monthly visitor, if you know what I mean. And male teachers seemed a little slow to catch on to the fact that you don't question a girl when she very suddenly needs to leave the classroom.

Whenever the teachers needed help setting up or tearing down they would always say, "I need a few of you strong young bucks to stay after class and help me . . ." This despite the fact that until tenth grade a lot of these young bucks were smaller than us robust does.

Boys had sports as a means to establish themselves in the pecking order of middle/high school society, but girls seemed to have only beauty as a means to establish themselves. In other words, popularity was determined by several factors for boys, but only by one factor for girls—were you considered pretty?

So far this has been "the chapter I can't write." I've spent about two months on it now. In the past fifteen minutes I have written and erased at least six paragraphs. The format of the book to this point has been as follows . . . I submit for your enjoyment humorous excerpts from my diary. You submit insightful comments that blow my diary away. I wax philosophical for a while, explaining to you why we girls behave the way we do. Then I give you that ironic twist from God's Word that completely convicts you and changes your life forever. Presto! Another chapter completed!

I find myself stuck on the waxing philosophical point here, so I'm going to have to take another route. Let's go with confession, and I'll hope that either some of you are like me and you will find this helpful to know you are not alone, or that the rest of you will be able to do what no other book or commentary has done for me yet . . . help me to understand why I struggle so badly with the fact that God's Word says I am "the weaker partner" (1 Peter 3:7) and that I am to "be silent" (1 Timothy 2:12).

First, I have to explain why these are struggles for me. If I simply didn't like the wording, and I had no trust in God, I could very quickly dismiss those verses, complain about Peter and Paul being chauvinists, and belligerently insist that I be given a pulpit somewhere. I could be like Thomas Jefferson and simply cut the portions of Scripture that I did not like right out of my Bible! The problem is . . . I fully believe in the authority of God's Word, the fact that Scripture is 100 percent without error, and in my husband's headship of our household.

Here's why I believe all of this is important for you. The Barna Group, a research organization designed to specifically study trends of the culture and the church, says that the church is losing America's youth; after the age of eighteen, when the average churched teenager goes off to college, she simply won't come back. In fact, only one of every three teens surveyed (out of roughly 3,000) reported that they intend to return regularly to a church body as an adult. The primary reason given is that churches are not doing enough to satisfy the need of teenagers for relevant relationship opportunities.[2] In other words, the primary reason for church attendance in the teen years is . . . "My friends are there." Other than these relationships, many teens simply do not see the church as useful.

Some of this drop in church attendance may be related to the kinds of things you will likely hear in your college classrooms. Odds are if you go to a secular university, the majority of your professors will be somewhat liberal. This is not to say you will not receive an excellent education— I know from experience that college by its very definition is a pretty amazing adventure! But one common objection to your church upbringing that you may hear is that the church has traditionally been "misogynistic," which is a fancy word that basically means "unfriendly toward women." And I have to warn you, if you are not prepared to remember that God is tickled silly pink, madly in love with you, and if you do not understand the role that God has set aside for women in the church community . . . you very well may fall prey to this misinformation.

**GOD'S DIARY**

I learned from your letters to me that a lot of you are flat-out thrilled with being a girl. I'm with you on that one. It just doesn't work to imagine otherwise, does it? I mean, we wouldn't begin to know what to talk about in the locker room. That's one of the greatest mysteries of the feminine life—what do guys talk about when no women are around? My suspicion sometimes is that everything reverts back to grunting. Then again, I'd like to believe that once in a while maybe all of the bravado gets set aside and guys talk about stuff similar to what we girls talk about. Maybe they discuss what they are looking for in a wife. Maybe they talk about really wanting kids one day, or how they think it's beautiful to watch a mom and her child snuggling or laughing together. Maybe when no one is looking they can comfort one another, pray for one another, and cry together. And if they can't do those things, I'm <u>totally</u> glad I'm a girl!

The last few scenarios I imagined above are traditionally more feminine than masculine. Women are set aside not only in traditional cultural stereo-types, but also in Scripture as having a nurturing and caretaking role. Perhaps the most famous passage on the role of women is found in Proverbs 31 . . .

> A wife of noble character who can find?
> She is worth far more than rubies. Her
> husband has full confidence in her and lacks

nothing of value. She brings him good, not harm, all the days of her life. She selects wool and flax and works with eager hands. She is like the merchant ships, bringing her food from afar. She gets up while it is still dark; she provides food for her family and portions for her servant girls. She considers a field and buys it; out of her earnings she plants a vineyard. She sets about her work vigorously; her arms are strong for her tasks. She sees that her trading is profitable, and her lamp does not go out at night. In her hand she holds the distaff and grasps the spindle with her fingers. She opens her arms to the poor and extends her hands to the needy. When it snows, she has no fear for her household; for all of them are clothed in scarlet. She makes coverings for her bed; she is clothed in fine linen and purple. Her husband is respected at the city gate, where he takes his seat among the elders of the land. She makes linen garments and sells them, and supplies the merchants with sashes. She is clothed with strength and dignity; she can laugh at the days to come. She speaks with wisdom, and faithful instruction is on her tongue. She watches over the affairs of her household and does not eat the bread of idleness. Her children arise and call her blessed; her husband also, and he praises her: "Many women do noble things, but you surpass them all." Charm is deceptive, and beauty is fleeting; but a woman who fears the LORD is to be praised. Give her the reward she has earned, and let her works bring her praise at the city gate.

Notice all of the varied roles of this superwoman! She obviously works and earns money, because she's out buying real estate with her earnings! She works so hard, as a matter of fact, that it's still dark when she gets up, and she has to burn her lamp well into the night. She is physically fit—strong arms. Basically, she's managing not only her own business and her family, but her husband's business as well . . . and he has total faith in her ability to do so! She is skilled both in the earning of money and in practical things such as the making of clothes and providing of food. She doesn't just write out a check to organizations that take care of the poor—she gets her hands dirty serving them. She's never going to appear on <u>Jerry Springer</u>, never going to embarrass her husband with her gossip or her poor public behavior. In fact, he's going to be honored by all of the other men because of her. He trusts her . . . she blesses him. It's a great partnership!

This is some important info if people are going to start telling us that the church wants women to remain weak and swept under a rug. I don't think such an argument could be supported using the Bible. Jesus had an absolutely revolutionary attitude toward women in His years on earth. Consider this . . . when Jesus was doing His public ministry, a woman was considered her husband's property. A woman often had no say in whom she married, and she could be divorced at will—even for a small offense such as burning dinner or preparing it late. In a court of law, women were not permitted to be legal witnesses . . . and yet whom did Jesus choose to be the first witness of His resurrection? Mary Magdalene, a woman. Though women were expected to serve men at a meal, Jesus corrected Martha and praised Mary . . . Martha, who was attempting to serve, and Mary, who was committed to sit at Jesus' feet and learn.

And consider this amazing factoid about Jesus' followers:

"After this, Jesus traveled about from one town and village to another, proclaiming the good news of the kingdom of God. The Twelve were with him, and also some women who had been cured of evil spirits and diseases: Mary (called Magdalene) from whom seven demons had come out; Joanna the wife of Cuza, the manager of Herod's household; Susanna; and many others. These women were helping to support them out of their own means." (Luke 8:1–3)

These women were the benefactors of Jesus' ministry! Out of their own earnings, their salaries, these working women were following Jesus around and financially supporting all that He did! But if you really want to see how revolutionary Jesus' attitude toward women was, check out these excerpts from some traditional Jewish texts . . .

"Rather should the words of the Torah be burned than entrusted to a woman . . . Whoever teaches his daughter the Torah is like one who teaches her obscenity."[3]

First century rabbis frequently prayed:

"I thank Thee, God, that I was not born a Gentile, a dog, or a woman."[4]

And finally, even though Paul and I are still at times wrestling over some of his commentaries on women in the church, it was Paul who wrote this:

"So in Christ Jesus you are all children of God through faith, for all of you who were baptized into Christ have clothed yourselves with Christ. There is neither Jew nor Gentile, neither slave nor free, neither male nor female, for you are all one in Christ Jesus."

(GALATIANS 3:26–28 TNIV)

It is crucial that we are content—no, even thrilled—about where God has placed us. Otherwise we end up in a place similar to Eve when she heard Satan's lie. "You will surely not die," the serpent said to the woman, "for God knows that when you eat of it your eyes will be opened, and you will be like God, knowing good and evil" (Genesis 3:4-5). Jesus is the head of the church. The man is the head of his house. Women are set loose to learn, manage, buy, sell, minister, support, provide, witness . . . Oh my goodness! We are supposed to do it all! But when we do it well, look at all the glory it brings—to God, to our church, to our husband and children (one day, right?). And remember, everything that God has put into a certain order, He has done so because when we keep things in that particular order we get to be part of something that is divine and holy rather than being part of something that is messed up, something full of drama and conflict, and something that sucks the life out of us!

If I'm going to be truly honest with you, I can give a name to that little chip that sits on my shoulder. It's called (sorry, this is a really long name) "But why do men get all the glory? Why can't women get a little of that glory? Why do men's sports break all of the attendance records and earn all of the money? Why are there more roles for men in movies than for women? Why don't girls get to initiate relationships? Why can't women sit on the elder board? Why, why, why?" And all along I miss the greater point of the order that God has established . . . Jesus gets the glory. Jesus gets the glory. Jesus gets the glory.

Not man, as I've so jealously believed. It's <u>not</u> a man's world after all. It's Jesus' world.

When you don't earn glory, what do you do? Back in 1991 a woman by the name of Wanda Webb Holloway made big headlines in the world of cheerleading . . . Actually, she simply made big headlines. Mrs. Holloway's daughter, Shanna, had failed to make her junior high cheerleading squad for two years in a row and Mrs. Holloway was not going to take any chances in year number three. She decided that her daughter's pretty rival, Amber, was to blame for Shanna's problems, so she attempted to hire a hit man to kill Amber's mother. Mrs. Holloway's hope was that Amber would be too distraught over her mother's death to perform well in cheerleading tryouts, thereby giving Shanna a chance to make the squad. Some news accounts say that Mrs. Holloway attempted to hire a hit on both Amber and her mother, but could not afford the double fee . . .

## MY STRUGGLE

Identify in the space below two
things in your life that you have been
tempted to <u>get the glory</u> for lately . . .

Now, let's take care of giving those things
to Jesus . . . where the glory belongs.

1. Create or locate within your home
something that can represent each of the
two things. It can be an actual object
(for me perhaps it would be one of my drum
sticks). It can also be a letter that you
write to God confessing on paper your
struggle to want glory for yourself.

2. Tell a friend, mentor, or your mom what it is that you are surrendering and about your struggle to receive glory or attention. Ask this person to help you think of a symbolic act of surrender that you can use with this object. It may be as simple as tossing the thing into the trash or driving to the dump together!

3. Pray together, agreeing that all glory and honor and power belong to God. Ask God to reveal any remnants of bitterness that remain in you—bitterness that you are not receiving the recognition you once sought.

CHAPTER 11

# THREE MAGIC WORDS:
## HELP FOR THE WOUNDED

I know how all you pet owners are, being one myself, and I don't mean to offend any of you zealous my-dog's-better-than-yours people, but . . . my dogs are better than yours. Seriously! I have probably the two best dogs on the face of the planet.

Biscuit came first—named after Seabiscuit the race horse, not the oddly shaped golden retriever in the children's books. (It is merely coincidence that my Biscuit happens to be a golden.) Scotti, as I like to call him, is the quirkiest dog. His favorite place to sleep is in the car . . . in the driveway . . . for hours at a time! He has a stuffed animal we call his "baby," and he carries it around with him everywhere. When he falls asleep at night he does so with his baby placed gently in his mouth. We have to keep him chained up because he likes to go visiting. My husband found him "visiting" the neighbors' pet duck the other day.

Hero arrived a bit after Biscuit. He's a Bernese mountain dog and probably has the best personality I've ever encountered in a dog. If dogs smiled out of happiness rather than submission, this little guy would be smiling nonstop. His life is one great adventure after another! We thought Biscuit was the cutest puppy ever, but along came Hero and suddenly Biscuit was living in the little guy's shadow. Everyone who sees this dog goes ga-ga over him.

There are some things about Scotti and Hero that strike me as funny. The first is that although both are eligible to be registered through the ACA (American Canine Association), we have not bothered to do so. They are licensed and microchipped, but officially they have no papers. In the world of dog show people, this makes them essentially no better than mongrels . . . mutts.

The second is that we got both dogs from the same breeder, and, as far as buying a dog goes, we did nearly everything wrong. We like to joke and say that the pups came from an "Amish puppy mill," which is not far from the truth. The breeder we bought from is indeed Amish and sells about ten different breeds of dog at any given time. We did no research on the seller and they asked no questions of us. I didn't begin looking for Hero until two weeks before we bought him—the experts say you should take three to six months to pick out the right dog and get on the waiting list of a reputable breeder. And yet somehow we ended up with two happy, healthy, and well-socialized dogs!

The point is this: These dogs are beautiful in every way and they don't even know it. Nor do they care. They do not live to have their fur brushed or their nails clipped. They hate baths and think that the worse they smell, the sexier they are. They say "hello" by sticking their noses in quite inappropriate places, and though not everyone likes them, they parade through life as though they were best in show.

What they do seem to know or have some kind of natural faith in is the fact that our family is tickled silly pink, madly in love with them. By the time they finish their short seven to ten years on this earth we will have invested any-where between $13,000 and $35,000 per dog! That's crazy! We buy them toys, food, treats . . . This week I even bought Hero some reindeer antlers for a little Christmas fun. And it looks like he needs a hernia operation—that's going to cost a penny or two.

I have pictures of the dogs on my phone that I make everyone look at. I kiss their noses (maybe not a great idea, but just try to stop me), talk baby talk to them, and take them on walks in the rain and freezing cold. One look and they melt my heart.

So let me remind you of this once again. Your Father is tickled silly pink, madly in love with you. Every gift you have comes from Him, and He is delighted to give all good things to you even though the cost for Him to do so was extraordinary.

He says you are beautiful, even though most of the time you don't realize it. You and I make decisions all the time to roll around in things that stink, and we think it's just great! Time and again He cleans and refreshes us, restoring us to His intended beauty.

How much better off would we be if we could approach all of our relationships with such simplistic trust? A lot of people will tell you that they have issues with trust. Maybe some of those trust issues are even reasonable. But I'm not talking about trusting in *people*. I'm saying, what if we had a simple trust in God, His love for us, and in His goodness? What if there really was some way for us to stop caring so much about the completely temporary nature of beauty and begin to do something crazy? How crazy? I'm talking about something pretty backwards here . . . What if we allowed God to define us rather than the world? God's

Word instead of *Teen People*. Prayer instead of gossip. People who build us up instead of that same old tired group of backbiters. Exchange the lies for some Truth.

Easier said than done? Maybe, but check this out first. My husband and I do some counseling for married couples and for those who are about to get married. I always do the session on conflict, because I have discovered the secret to living at peace with other people. Does it work 100 percent of the time? No, because people do not always cooperate, including myself. But if we used these three magic words every time we encountered conflict and insecurity . . . well, conflict and insecurity would all but disappear. Are you ready? Here they are:

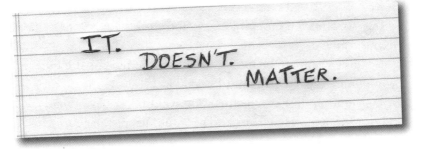

IT. DOESN'T. MATTER.

Here's how it works. I want you to think right now of the last three fights you had with your parents or with a friend, or of the last three times your feelings were hurt. Would you be able to tell me the specifics of those three times? What were the details of the fight? What exactly was said to hurt you? Most couples in counseling laugh and tell us it's funny, because they can remember fighting but they just can't remember what the fight was about. Sometimes they argue about what they argued over . . .

When we are hurt physically our first reaction is to grab and cover the wound. It is no different emotionally. Because

I am not a research scientist I can only speak for myself, but I think this is a universal reaction—pain makes me want to lash out and return pain to whatever has hurt me. It is not usually a rational response. I have attempted in the past to inflict pain on such things as a rocking chair that hurt my toe and a bike that threw me off on a gravel road. My reactions to people have not necessarily contained more rational thought—I remember one time my husband hurt my feelings (I have no recollection what was said or done) so I decided I would show him! I went and sat in our walk-in closet for about fifteen minutes and I did not answer though he walked about the house calling my name! Hah! What brilliant strategy!

When I address pain I merely react. When I address the offense, the result is much different. Most things that are said to or about me are of little consequence. Yes, I am aware that "sticks and stones may break my bones but words will never hurt me" is one of the greatest lies ever perpetuated in this world. But in many cases we allow things to hurt and offend that just do not matter. The proof of this is in the fact that within a period of twenty-four hours we forget the content of our battles—we only remember that we have been wounded.

I have actually had some amazing success by applying the three magic words to conflict in my own relationships. Do I get wounded by others? You bet. But I've learned to stop and think about what was said or done before I clutch at the wound and strike out in retribution. It stops me from doing things I later regret . . . and it stops me from believing a *lot* of lies! Remember in chapter 4 we reviewed a verse from James that says we fight and quarrel because we do not get what we want? It's so true! What else *could* we fight about besides the desire to see things go the way we want them to go? And that's where the words IT DOESN'T MATTER come so perfectly into play.

I want things to look like A.

My friend wants things to look like B.

She is afraid she won't get her way, so she goes behind my back to get support from others.

I feel like choking her, because that was embarrassing. It alienated me from the other girls. I feel stupid—I stick out like a sore thumb.

Then I realize I'm reacting to the pain.

If things look like B this time, is that really so bad?

I go to my friend and say, "Hey, what you did
kind of hurt my feelings."

Chances are, she's going to apologize.
She was reacting, too.

Suddenly, neither of us care so much
if it's A or B. It doesn't matter.

All I can tell you is I've applied the above principle
numerous times with friends, employers, my husband, my
kids, my mom . . . It always turns out pretty sweet in the
end. This comes with a disclaimer, of course. There are bad
people out there. There are people who will never concede
to do things any way other than their own. There are people
who want what goes against God's very truth. There are
people who will deceive, connive, wound . . . and never seem
to feel the least bit bad about it. I have three magic words for
dealing with these people, too.

TURN. AND. RUN!!

There are some people it's best not to waste our time on.

For the most part, I guess I want to be like Biscuit and Hero. They're the two best dogs on the face of the planet. I want to trust in the goodness and care of my Master. I want it to be okay when things don't go my way. I don't have to be the alpha dog. And I want to get up with my tail wagging even after I've been hurt. In the long run, it doesn't matter. My Daddy is tickled silly pink, madly in love with me . . . and there's a big juicy pig's ear waiting for me at home . . .

PRIVATE
STAY OUT!

# CHAPTER NOTES

## CHAPTER 1: IT WAS A GOOD YEAR . . .

1. http://dictionary.reference.com/browse/adversary

2. Matthew Henry, *Matthew Henry's Commentary on the Whole Bible, Complete and Unabridged* (Peabody, MA: Hendrickson, 1991).

## CHAPTER 2: MY WORLD . . . YOUR WORLD

1. Department of Health and Human Services (US), Administration on Children, Youth and Families. "Child Maltreatment 2003" [online]. Washington: Government Printing Office; 2005. Available from URL: www.acf.hhs.gov/programs/cb/pub/cm03/

2. B.S. Fisher, F.T. Cullen, M.G. Turner, "The sexual victimization of college women," Washington: Department of Justice (US), National Institute of Justice; 2000. Publication No. NCJ 182369.

3. P. Tjaden, N. Thoennes, "Full report of the prevalence, incidence, and consequences of violence against women: findings from the national violence against women survey." Washington: National Institute of Justice; 2000. Report NCJ 183781.

4. www.cbsnews.com/stories/2006/02/06/eveningnews/main1286130.shtml

5. "Sexuality, Contraception, and the Media," American Academy of Pediatrics Committee on Public Education, January, 2001.

6. "New look at TV sex and violence," *National Catholic Register*, 16–22 April 2000.

7. Marilyn Elias, "TV Might Rush Teens Into Sex," *USA Today*, http://www.usatoday.com/news/health/2004-09-06-teens-tv-sex-usat_x.htm .

## CHAPTER 3: BOY CRAZY—LOOKING FOR ATTENTION

1. Rick Warren, *The Purpose Driven Life* (Grand Rapids: Zondervan, 2001), 67.

## CHAPTER 4: GIRLFRIENDS—LOOKING FOR ACCEPTANCE

1. http://home.comcast.net/~motherteresasite/prayers.html

## CHAPTER 5: SELF-ESTEEM—LOOKING FOR HOPE

1. Jeff Schewe, "Kate Doesn't Like Photoshop—Digital Ethics," *Photoshop News*, http://photoshopnews.com/2005/04/03/kate-doesnt-like-photoshop

2. Donna Freydkin, "Doctored Cover Photos Add Up to Controversy," *USA Today*, http://www.usatoday.com/life/2003-06-16-covers_x.htm

3. Esther Addley, "Faking It," *Guardian*, http://www.guardian.co.uk/women/story/0,3604,871839,00.html

4. http://www.babycentre.co.uk/preconception/activelytrying/howbabiesaremade/

## CHAPTER 6: MEAN GIRLS—LOOKING FOR POWER

1. Rosalind Wiseman, *Queen Bees and Wannabes* (New York: Three Rivers Press, 2002).

## CHAPTER 8: REBELLION—LOOKING FOR INDEPENDENCE

1. Dr. James Dobson, "Cultivating Good Attitude," *Focus on the Family*, http://www.family.org.my/detail.asp?idx=62&media=tblnewspaper

CHAPTER 9: MOM WAS RIGHT—LOOKING FOR HEALING

1. Craig Jutila, "Teaching Children to Walk Like You," Purpose Driven Ministries, http://www.pastors.com/article.asp?ArtID=9065

2. Sean McEvoy, "Man-To-Man: An Interview with Donald Miller," Crosswalk, http://www.crosswalk.com/1395535/tpage3.html

3. Howard S. Hoffman, "Imprinting: A Brief Description," The Animated Software Company, http://www.animatedsoftware.com/family/howardsh/imprint.htm

4. Mark Twain, "Old Times on the Mississippi," *Atlantic Monthly*, 1874.


CHAPTER 10: GLAD I'M A GIRL?—
LOOKING FOR A FUTURE

1. Charles Murray, "The Inequality Taboo," *Opinion Journal*, http://www.opinionjournal.com/extra/?id=110007391

2. The Barna Group, "Teens Change Their Tune Regarding Self and Church," http://www.barna.org/FlexPage.aspx?Page=BarnaUpdate&BarnaUpdateID=111

3. Rabbi Eliezer, *Mishnah, Sotah 3:4.*

4. Doug Clark, "Jesus and Women," *Enrichment Journal*, http://enrichmentjournal.ag.org/200102/024_jesus_and_women.cfm